Cohen and Cassirer, which considered him a thinker primarily concerned with epistemology.

RICHARD KRONER *is Professor Emeritus at the University of Kiel, Germany, and at Union Theological Seminary. He is also Permanent Visiting Professor at Temple University and at the University of Bern; has taught at Freiburg, Dresden, and Oxford; and delivered the Gifford Lectures at St. Andrews in 1939–40. Dr. Kroner is the author of a monumental two-volume study of the development of German idealism,* Von Kant bis Hegel. *Among his other works are* The Religious Function of Imagination; The Primacy of Faith *(Gifford Lectures);* How Do We Know God? Culture and Faith *(University of Chicago Press, 1951); and an introduction and translations in Hegel's* Early Theological Writings *(with T. M. Knox [University of Chicago Press, 1948]).*

JOHN E. SMITH *is Assistant Professor of Philosophy at Yale University.*

KANT'S WELTANSCHAUUNG

KANT'S WELTANSCHAUUNG

By

RICHARD KRONER

English Translation by

JOHN E. SMITH

THE UNIVERSITY OF CHICAGO PRESS

An authorized translation of *Kants Weltanschauung*
(Tübingen, 1914) with revisions by the author

Library of Congress Catalog Number: 56-6640

THE UNIVERSITY OF CHICAGO PRESS, CHICAGO 37
Cambridge University Press, London, N.W. 1, England
The University of Toronto Press, Toronto 5, Canada

ⓒ *1956 by The University of Chicago. Copyright under
the International Copyright Union, 1956. Published 1956
Composed and printed by* THE UNIVERSITY OF CHICAGO
PRESS, *Chicago, Illinois, U.S.A.*

Foreword

EVERYONE familiar with Kant's thought will admit that he is a difficult writer; to follow him through his intricate arguments and his complexity of expression constantly taxes the reader. Because of this, those reading and teaching Kant have frequently tended to stress every detail; they have attempted to catch his meaning by devoting the most painstaking attention to each passage. The result has been an overemphasis upon the details of Kant's system, particularly on the early part of the first *Critique,* and the consequent loss of a total perspective upon the Kantian philosophy. It is impossible to overestimate the confusion which follows; there are many who have mastered at least the rudiments of Kant's analysis of human cognition but who still remain largely in the dark about the more basic questions which his epistemological inquiries were intended to answer. Thus there are few who can contemplate the details of Kant's theory fully aware that his entire epistemology was intended to decide whether man, with his limited capacities, is capable of resolving the philosophical problems set forth in the "Transcendental Dialectic" of the first

Critique. Frequently the problems of the third section of the *Critique of Pure Reason* are left to one side with the result that the basic meaning of Kant's criticism of knowledge is lost. Yet in spite of his rejection of speculative metaphysics, the fact remains that Kant's main concern was with the plight of human reason when confronted with questions which it cannot avoid but which it also cannot answer. The analysis of knowledge is not an isolated affair but a preliminary to determine the scope of human knowledge and the validity of moral activity. When this fact is forgotten, the study of Kant degenerates into piecemeal consideration of epistemological details, and Kant's basic perspective is lost. It is a case of our having lost sight of the main purpose of Kant's thought because we have taken too myopic a view of his philosophy.

Richard Kroner's book, *Kant's Weltanschauung*,[1] will help to rectify this error. Drawing upon his vast knowledge of Kant's writing, he succeeds in setting forth the main drift of Kant's thought—Kant's basic philosophical perspective. It is this perspective which is meant by the term "Weltanschauung," a term we have decided to retain in the English translation, partly because it now has considerable currency in America, but chiefly because no English word or phrase adequately

1. First published in German by J. C. B. Mohr (Tübingen: Paul Siebeck, 1914).

expresses what the author has in mind. Kroner seeks to draw together all strands of Kant's thought so that the critical philosophy can be seen as a whole and as a sustained attempt to communicate one idea—the primacy of the willing subject over all knowledge and all speculative constructions of reality. This one idea, as the reader will discover, represents Kroner's interpretation of Kant's Weltanschauung.

Kantian scholarship of the past century has been so vast and varied that it would be a matter of great surprise if different schools of interpretation had not developed. The so-called Marburg school is the one best known to English readers, and even those unfamiliar with the details have heard of the "back to Kant" movement associated with such commentators as Natorp, Cohen, and Cassirer. Less known in this country is the interpretation of the Heidelberg school, associated with the names of Rickert and Windelband. Kroner's book is representative of this latter point of view. Those who participated in the "zurück zu Kant" movement were inclined to regard post-Kantian speculation as misguided and thoroughly un-Kantian, a view which in turn led them to strip Kant of all vestiges of metaphysical thought and thereby reduce him to a thinker concerned only with epistemology. For the Marburg school, going back to Kant meant going back to epistemological philosophy and completely away from speculative questions. The Heidelberg interpretation, on the other hand, while it also in a sense went "back to Kant," was more concerned to discover the fundamental moral questions which Kant's critical philosophy attempted to answer.

Thus in *Kant's Weltanschauung* Kroner does not simply sweep aside Kant's successors as illegitimate heirs to his thought, but he shows how Kant in his own way tried to solve the same questions which Fichte, Schelling, and Hegel had attempted to solve by metaphysical speculation. The principal point established by Kroner's analysis is that for Kant the will, in the form of the individual willing subject, is supreme in human life and that as actual will it is superior to all knowing and superior to all speculative metaphysics, even to those in which will itself is made the central principle. Kant's Weltanschauung, according to Kroner, is the insight that the actualization of human freedom in moral action is man's highest ability and duty, and that only in moral action itself do the dualities posed by speculative reason disappear.

From this ethical perspective, Kroner interprets Kant's epistemological dualism, phenomenalism, and subjectivism, and instead of regarding these features of the first *Critique* as aspects of a self-contained theory of knowledge, he aims to show how each is required by Kant's ultimate conviction that morality is superior to metaphysical knowledge. This means that ethical considerations are first in importance and that far from being an appendage intended to supplement a skeptical epistemology, the ethical outlook actually determines the Kantian theory of knowledge.

In addition to being an important contribution in itself, Kroner's interpretation serves to focus attention once more upon the whole outlook of Kant and to remind us that such a total perspective is operative throughout Kant's thought.

Richard Kroner, formerly Professor in the University of Kiel, came to America in 1940. Since then he has taught at the Union Theological Seminary in New York and more recently at Temple University, in addition to lecturing at Vassar College, Yale University, and other institutions of higher learning. He is the author of an excellent little book, *The Religious Function of Imagination,* and also of *The Primacy of Faith,* the Gifford Lectures for 1939, as well as *Culture and Faith,* a revised and enlarged version of an original philosophical system published by him in 1928 under the title: *Die Selbstverwirklichung des Geistes.* His monumental two volume interpretation of the development of German Idealism, *Von Kant bis Hegel,* has, unfortunately, never been translated into English. When this is done it will greatly benefit English readers studying German thought.

Finally, a word about the translation itself. In most places the English follows the German closely, but in others, notably chapter iii on "Ethical Subjectivism," Kroner has made radical revisions. At times he has shortened sentences and at others he has recast the original completely. The entire translation has been checked by the author, but final responsibility for any errors in translation or infelicitous expressions rests with the translator alone.

I am indebted to my wife for verifying many of the notes, and especially to Professor Lewis W. Beck of the University of Rochester who has kindly given of his time to prepare an index and to check the proofs; without his help the appearance of the book would most surely have been delayed.

It is hoped that a small book on Kant in English which is both intelligible and suggestive will not only provide an over-all viewpoint for those already familiar with Kant but will also stimulate others to begin study of the Kantian philosophy with some understanding of the more basic questions behind Kant's formidable analysis of the structure of human knowledge and the goal of human freedom.

JOHN E. SMITH

NOTE.—The notes to the chapters are by J. E. Smith, except the note to chapter v, which is by the author.

Table of Contents

INTRODUCTION 1

  I. ETHICAL VOLUNTARISM 6

 II. ETHICAL DUALISM 30

III. ETHICAL SUBJECTIVISM 61

IV. ETHICAL PHENOMENALISM 92

 V. PRIMACY OF THE PRACTICAL 108

INDEX 119

Introduction

IT IS of the essence in a philosophical system to proceed by means of demonstration, to supply objective reasons and not to depend on subjective motives, feelings, and conjectures in place of argument. Nevertheless, the comprehension of the rational, logical, and objective character of the concepts in a system can be facilitated if one penetrates the spirit and ethos alive in the system. When I refer to the spirit and ethos of Kant's philosophy, I do not intend to depict the character of the inner life of Kant as the biographer might do, but rather I intend to concentrate on what should be called "Kant's Weltanschauung," which originates not from Kant as a person but from Kant as the author of one of the world's great philosophical systems. The ethical and religious views of Kant are, for this purpose, a better source than his epistemological theories. His ethical and religious views are more deeply rooted in the philosophical center of his personality and therefore of his Weltanschauung.

Two great cultural powers are at the very foundation of the Kantian philosophy: natural science and moral life. The manner in which Kant pits these two powers against each other constitutes the dynamics of his system. For in their reality he sees the foci around which all philosophical thought moves, and he regards it as of the utmost importance to co-ordinate the two within a system. His entire philosophy receives its particular tone from a twofold insight. On the one hand, along with modern rationalists since Descartes and Galileo, he sees, in the exactitude of mathematical knowledge, the pattern and ideal of all theoretical study of reality; on the other hand, in spite of his full appreciation of scientific truth, he does not accord it any metaphysical significance. Kant is of the opinion that the point of contact between man and the supersensible and eternal sphere is to be discerned in the facts of man's moral life, in his self-determination, and in the laws of his moral will; for it is on these laws that the dignity and freedom of man rest. Putting together the two evaluations (natural science and moral life), the denial of a metaphysical knowledge of the supersensible world must inevitably result. Only mathematical relations are knowable, and they are the objects which the mechanical and physical sciences can successfully treat. The world in which we as moral beings act and pursue our ends obviously cannot be penetrated by mathematical knowledge; therefore this world cannot be grasped in its reality by any theoretical means. The supersensible and eternal world is accessible only through moral activity; we are in the process of building it by living in accordance with moral laws. We make ourselves citizens of this world by overcoming the impact of the sensible world and in learning to control it by the moral self. The supersensible world of which we are members, inasmuch as we are conscious of our selfhood and act as free agents in the world of sense, can never be understood by theoretical means. It is nature only that can be objectively investigated and grasped by the natural sciences. In this sense, man as an agent confronts nature merely as the raw material of his activity, as something which can be molded according to his purpose. Exact mathematical knowledge is therefore exalted by Kant, for such knowledge alone represents the true science of reality, and it alone produces objective truth about its object. Yet, at the same time, the metaphysical value of this knowledge is rated low. Science does not penetrate into the supersensible, the infinite, and the unlimited; science conveys theoretical information only about a subordinate part of the world, a part whose metaphysical insignificance appears most clearly when we consider that from it originates just those sensuous impulses and desires which undermine the dominion of moral reason.

The abrogation of the comprehension of the supersensible world thus originates from the double appraisal: the theoretical appraisal of the mathematical-physical method and the metaphysical appraisal of the moral will. If Kant had attempted to extend this method, which he deemed to be the only legitimate and feasible theoretical method for knowing reality, to the world in which we live as active beings (as indeed the disciples of materialism and naturalism would like to do), then he would have been compelled to abandon the respect he had for moral life. Within a nature interpreted mathematically no morality can exist, because there every action loses its meaning; in such a world the will cannot set any purpose for itself, since mathematics alone orders and determines all things in its own inexorable and absolute way. If Kant, on the other hand, had admitted the possibility of a theoretical metaphysics of the supersensible world, he would have been compelled to give up the thesis that the mathematical and scientific method alone can comprehend reality in a theoretical way. Such a theoretical metaphysics would necessarily have tended to encroach upon nature as well, so that mathematical science would have been relegated to a place of secondary importance.

Kant maintains the non-metaphysical but theoretical validity of mathematical science and the non-theoretical but metaphysical validity of the moral life. He thereby apportions the value of theoretical knowledge and the value of the metaphysical and supersensible to the two cultural realms especially precious to him: mathematical science and the moral life. In this way he attempted to do justice to both realms without destroying the one by means of the other.

I

Ethical Voluntarism

Iɴ ʜɪs brilliant lectures on Kant, Simmel[1] defends the thesis that Kant basically is a radical intellectualist and that the emphasis placed by him on the moral life in the last analysis results in an intellectualistic interpretation of the will. Simmel's thesis is correct with respect to certain passages in Kant's ethics; however, if one takes into account the general spirit of Kantian philosophy one cannot call it intellectualistic. The great originality of his philosophy rests (as Windelband, above all, has pointed out) on the fact that it accords the highest place within the totality of the human consciousness and within the totality of Weltanschauung not to the intellect but to the will. Kant's philosophy is voluntaristic.

This statement may perhaps mislead, in so far as modern man immediately connects with the term "voluntarism" the metaphysics associated with Schopenhauer. But nothing of this sort is to be found in Kant.

1. Georg Simmel (1858–1918), German sociologist and philosopher, concerned mainly with social and moral philosophy.

The whole Kantian Weltanschauung centers, not around the will in general, but around the morally good will or around the individual will which subjects itself to the moral law. Kant, moreover, does not regard this moral will as the hidden core, the substance of the world; he absolutely renounces the task of building up a scientific philosophy of the supersensible world out of the facts of moral life. He merely states that moral life points to the supersensible world. Hence, if one understands by voluntarism a metaphysics in which the will is the center of reality, then Kant's philosophy is no voluntarism; Kant denies that knowledge of the will has any speculative significance. Schopenhauer's metaphysical and speculative voluntarism is infinitely more intellectualistic than Kant's philosophy.

Kant's Weltanschauung emphasizes that the metaphysical significance of the will cannot be adequately expressed in a theory of the will but only by the activity of the will itself in its moral capacity. Kant holds that metaphysics as a theoretical science is impossible precisely because the metaphysical dignity of human life rests in that activity and capacity. All metaphysics is necessarily intellectualistic and consequently exalts the intellect over the will. He, on the other hand, who declares that the will is supreme has to conclude that the nature of things is incomprehensible. Of course, philosophical knowledge of the moral will is not denied by the rejection of a voluntaristic metaphysics, as Kant's ethics shows. But such ethical knowledge must confine itself to understanding the nature of morality, and it must also try to make the respective claims of natural science and morality compatible. Such an undertaking Kant regards as the main task of philosophy. He refuses, however, to expand ethics into a metaphysics of the will. We shall see later that such an expansion beyond the boundaries of ethics constitutes, in Kant's view, the very principle of all speculative metaphysics. The intellect must yield its authority to that of the will, for the will can only play its own metaphysical role in a world which is not fully comprehensible. The will can play its metaphysical role, not in so far as it is taken as the essence of the world, but only to the extent that it is the principle of action aiming at the good; for action is meaningless in an absolutely comprehended world. Thus Kant's philosophy is one of ethical voluntarism.

In Kant the metaphysical takes on an entirely new significance. It permeates actual life in a much more profound way than would be possible in a voluntaristic metaphysics. Such a metaphysics recognizes desire and will as the very nature of things or in Kantian terms the "thing-in-itself"; but according to such a metaphysics man is not able to comprehend the thing-in-itself by desiring and willing. Rather it is the intellect, without regard to the will, which discovers its metaphysical nature and function. Every beast is moved by desire and according to Schopenhauer even the stone has a will that draws it to the ground; yet without Schopenhauer's metaphysics it is not possible to ascribe metaphysical dignity to the desire of the beast or to the will of the stone. The will takes on its metaphysical significance only as a principle in a system, that is, only if it is no longer mere will but is transformed into thought, in short, into philosophy.

But by this transformation voluntarism is itself changed into intellectualism. If, on the contrary, it is true that the metaphysical dimension of man is to be found in actual willing rather than in knowledge of the will, in the deed and not in the theory, then the real value of the metaphysical resides wholly in willing and doing and not in knowing. Consequently, the metaphysical dimension of man must no longer be sought in willing as such but only in moral willing. For if the will is no longer the principle of a metaphysical cosmology, it must be conceived as requiring a new quality which constitutes its metaphysical function and dignity.

If the metaphysical no longer manifests itself by its

power of unifying the manifold of appearances, if it is no longer the ultimate ground of both the being and knowledge of this manifold, then an analogous meaning for the life of the will must be ascribed to it, which gives us the right to declare that this life itself represents what we vainly sought in theory. Once the possibility of making the will the center of a metaphysical theory is dismissed, then the will can be conceived as making itself the center—the ultimate center and unity. Such a will would then attain to the high rank of the metaphysical or supersensible. The metaphysical, in so far as man is able to reach it, is not reserved to those who attend to it by means of philosophical intuition or knowledge; rather, it is open to all those who subordinate their will to the supreme and ultimate end. This end transcends the finite wishes and desires of the individual and unites him with all mankind. Instead of assuming that philosophy with its logical deduction knows the will to be the essence of the world, we must acknowledge that philosophy only learns what the concept of the metaphysical means from moral will and practical reason: ethics thus replaces metaphysics.

The will obtains its metaphysical dignity not through the instrumentality of metaphysics but through itself, in so far as it directs itself toward the good. Metaphysical knowledge would only attribute to the will something that the will itself could not attain by willing, namely, the quality of being the substance and the supreme principle of all things. The quality, on the contrary, which constitutes the metaphysical function of the will can be attained by willing and only by willing. Of course, ethics has to conceive this quality, and only in so far as it is conceived can it be called metaphysical. But, even so, the value of the metaphysical does not depend on this act of conceiving; rather it depends on the moral achievement with which ethics is concerned. In short, all depends on the actuality and not on the theory of the deed. The metaphysical, consequently, is not what is universal and identical in all theoretical knowledge but what is universal and identical in willing. Ethics conceives this as the form of the moral will, as the law not of a Supersensible Being but as the law of the Supersensible Willing.

There is no metaphysical law of nature, but it is the moral law within our will which is the metaphysical law. It is the law of the supernatural or supersensible world. He who obeys that law rises above the level of the world of sense. He rises above that necessity and order which govern nature; he enters the realm of freedom and reason which transcends the phenomenal sphere.

Cognition of what is never enables finite beings to

transcend the limits of the senses and thus of finitude and limitation; this cognition is confined to the narrow circle encompassed by space and time. There is no ontological vision possible that would surpass these boundaries and penetrate into the precinct of the non-spatial and the non-temporal, i.e., the eternal. By the subordination of the will to the moral law, however, man is able to free himself from the compulsion of natural necessity. If the will acts, motivated not by sense impressions, impulses, and desires, that is to say, by man's nature, but out of respect for the moral law, then it performs the miracle of mastering natural necessity. In this way the will subjugates nature and establishes a metaphysical order beyond it. With this in mind it is instructive to compare the three voluntarists, Kant, Schopenhauer, and Nietzsche.

Of the three, Schopenhauer least deserves the title of "voluntarist," if one understands by voluntarism a Weltanschauung which locates the metaphysical center of the human being in his will and his act. Schopenhauer can rather be called an intellectualist. His metaphysics ennobles the will by means of philosophical speculation but not through its own end and objective. The will in his view cannot will the metaphysical because it is itself the metaphysical by its own nature and not by its willing. It is being not willing which makes the will metaphysical. That being even Schopenhauer cannot help identifying with the philosophical concept of the will, although he claims to be an "irrationalist." This ontological identification becomes especially clear if one bears in mind that, according to Schopenhauer, the metaphysical act in particular is not to be found in willing but, on the contrary, in the denial and negation of the will. Whereas Kant insists that man attains metaphysical rank only if he exalts his will morally, i.e., if he actively participates in the founding of the kingdom of reason: Schopenhauer teaches, on the contrary, that man reaches his highest stage only in willing not to will at all.

Not a mode of willing (as in Kant) but the capacity of not willing distinguishes man from all other beings and enables him to accomplish his metaphysical task. The condition for such an accomplishment is, of course, the knowledge and acceptance of Schopenhauer's metaphysics or, at least, an intuitive comprehension of its truth; in other words, the condition is a state of knowledge as well as of insight. Only the man who knows, not the man who wills, succeeds in negating the will. The intellectual contemplation of the will as the nature of all things and as the source of the human tragedy is the liberating act, namely, the act which liberates man from acting altogether. According to Kant, moral willing frees us from subservience to desire and sensuality, while reason makes the will free. According to Schopenhauer, reason makes us free from all willing.

Schopenhauer begins as a voluntarist but he ends as an intellectualist. The will is not, as he first maintained, the absolute substance of the world, otherwise man could never overcome it. The ultimate and absolute is non-willing and non-acting; it is, as Schopenhauer says, nothingness. A voluntarist, in the Kantian sense, can never proclaim that the world is ultimately tragic, he can never make nothingness his God, that is only possible for a quietist, a Buddhist, like Schopenhauer. It is in accord with this conclusion that Schopenhauer teaches that life and will are, in the last analysis, due to a guilt which is punished by suffering and death. In the end the will is not at all the true thing-in-itself, but rather the consequence of a metaphysical meta-voluntaristic, meta-ethical fall, a falling away from the true absolute which is nothingness. It is characteristic of the man that he says, "one can conceive of our life as an unnecessary and disturbing episode in the blessed calm of nothingness." If existence is completely meaningless, then what meaning can be given to willing? Had Schopenhauer's thought as expressed in the last book of *The World as Will and Idea* been made the starting point of his thinking, consistency would have led him to maintain that nothingness is the very essence of the world, while will and idea are merely illusions woven by the veil of *maya*. He whose eyes can pierce this veil liberates himself from illusions; he beholds the pure absolute nothingness, the things-in-themselves without any intervening medium. At the end of his work Schopenhauer comes to this conclusion. He who is delivered from the will and beholds the truth, that is, the world as will and idea, turns into nothingness which in turn becomes true being. Only as long as we cling to existence do we believe that true nothingness, namely, the world, is something. "Behind our existence lies something else which is accessible to us only if we have shaken off this world."[2]

Schopenhauer is so deeply rooted in intellectualism that, in the last analysis, he not only abandons the will, but even voluntarism itself, his very metaphysics of the will. Kant had already fought against this thesis even before Schopenhauer had expressed it. Kant once said that "the brooding man" who attempts to liberate himself from all the evils of this world gets immersed in mysticism, "where his reason no longer understands

2. R. B. Haldane and J. Kemp (trans.), *The World as Will and Idea* (London: Kegan Paul, 1906), I, 523.

itself and its own intentions but prefers to roam about instead of confining itself within its proper boundaries as behooves an intellectual inhabitant of a sensuous world. Out of this misbehavior the monster system of Laotse arises, teaching that the highest good consists in nothingness, i.e., in the feeling of being swallowed up by the abyss of the godhead . . . only in order to enable man to enjoy eternal calm and thus to reach the alleged blessed end of all things. This nothingness, truly conceived, is a concept which annihilates all understanding and in which thought itself arrives at its end."[3]

As compared with Schopenhauer, Nietzsche is a much more consistent voluntarist. He does not maintain that the will is the essence of the world. Rather he denies that this essence can be known and confines himself to proclaiming the importance of willing as such. He is a staunch defender of the will and makes willing an end in itself. Therefore he teaches that the highest expression of the will is the will to power, for he who risks all for the sake of willing is bound to desire the power to overcome all obstacles which would thwart him. Will to power is will to boundless willing; it is willing to the highest degree. However, this affirmation of the will no longer has the support of Scho-

3. "Das Ende aller Dinge" (1794), *Gesammelte Schriften* (Akademie Ausg.), VIII, 335 f.

penhauer's voluntaristic metaphysic, and it remains suspended in air.

Affirmation of the will may have a solid foundation within a voluntaristic metaphysics. It may also be meaningful in such a system to regard a great amount of will power as valuable and significant. If the world is essentially will, it is conceivable that the possessor of a great will can express the essence of the world more adequately than one with a meager will, and that the stronger will would be in greater harmony with the supersensible nature of all things. Of course, such an exaltation of willing would, even within a voluntaristic metaphysic, be possible only by means of a previous intellectualization of the will. Thus Spinoza gives metaphysical prominence to the powerful will but only by identifying will and intellect according to his formula, "will and intellect are one and the same thing."

Nietzsche, however, discards every metaphysical interpretation of the will precisely because he is the true voluntarist; how then can he still assert that willing is meaningful? How can he ascribe any value to the naked insatiable desire? Why does he give so much importance to such a desire? After all, it is innate as a natural force in all living beings, and as will to power it is in all human beings the most common and widespread fact. If it is true that the philosopher should grant particular significance to the will and that the very meaning of the world is bound up with the question, what should we will, then man's will must be of ultimate importance. It is not mere quantity of will that makes the will significant and meaningful, for a very strong but valueless will is obviously worse than a weak one. Only the quality, not the quantity, only value and direction, not strength and force of will, can entitle the philosopher to give will the primacy over knowledge.

An intellectualistic metaphysics lurks behind even Nietzsche's affirmation of the will, but this metaphysics endows the mere will with a value, a value which the will as such does not possess at all. The following idea is behind Nietzsche's affirmation of the will: the sensible world alone really and truly exists, there is no supersensible, there is nothing metaphysical. From this idea the conclusion immediately follows that the best we can and should do in this world is to enjoy it as much as possible. We are not to be deceived by the empty consolation of a world to come: all we have to gain we must gain here. This antimetaphysical metaphysics, born out of opposition to Schopenhauer's nothingness and deifying the earth and everything earthly instead of nothingness, is indeed able to bestow a value upon the will. To the voluntaristically minded thinker, willing, of whatever sort, is better than denial of the will. Every activity is more precious than a boring inactivity or the sweet calm of nothingness exalted by Schopenhauer. The exaggerated emphasis Nietzsche puts upon the will and upon existence as such is thus to be interpreted as the voluntaristic reaction against the intellectualist and Buddhist Schopenhauer, just as Nietzsche's campaign against Christianity is, in the last analysis, a campaign against Schopenhauer's ethics of compassion.[4] Every reason to glorify the will to power disappears if one disregards the motive behind this campaign. The whole basis of Nietzsche's voluntarism is abolished when his metaphysics of this life is no longer set in opposition to Schopenhauer's metaphysics of the life to come.

Only those who abandon the metaphysical (though also antimetaphysical) dogma that there is nothing at all but this visible universe can enter into Kant's Weltanschauung. Only they can take a stand with Kant who recognize that moral action harbors a value of its own which is dependent upon itself alone and includes the appreciation of a supersensible good en-

4. Cf. Simmel's instructive book, *Schopenhauer und Nietzsche* (Leipzig, 1920).

tirely independent of earthly successes. Everyone is capable of this. No one wants to be a scoundrel or a villain; everyone despises wickedness as such and not only because he fears the disadvantages of evil behavior. Everyone pays tribute to an unconditional value, a value which is not derived from any higher value but is itself the highest. Only at times the sophisticated intellect fancies itself to have dispensed with such an allegiance or to have explained it away. "Concerning those ideas," says Schiller, "which prevail in the moral part of the Kantian system, only the philosophers disagree, all other human beings have always found themselves in agreement." In his moral analysis Kant reveals himself as the true voluntarist who relies more on what the will and the heart directly pronounce than on any analysis a metaphysic could provide.

All analyses center around finite and conditional relations. In morality, however, the unconditional is at stake. It is noteworthy that even Nietzsche has to acknowledge this sometimes. In his book, *The Joyful Science (Fröhliche Wissenschaft)*, he raises the question, why do we want science and truth at all? He feels obliged to admit that this want does not always contribute to our welfare on earth, and that it may even cause great harm, and thus he concludes that the will to truth at least involves a kind of metaphysical faith which includes recognition of a world beyond that of life and nature. Nietzsche puts all these thoughts under the significant heading: "To what extent are we still religious?"

Kant's Weltanschauung is rooted precisely in that metaphysical faith which Nietzsche mentions here. Unfortunately Nietzsche did not even keep this faith to the end but denied truth and science themselves and thus destroyed the meaning of his own words. Kant, on the other hand, regards this faith as the firm ground on which we must stand in order to characterize man's position in the world and the relation of the world to ourselves.

Kant holds that the recognition of an imperative, guiding us not only when we seek the truth but guiding our will as its highest measure and goal, brings us nearer to the ultimate meaning of the world than any speculative or theoretical knowledge possibly could. If you follow the voice of your conscience, if you fulfil your duty, however large it may loom, then you will penetrate deeper into the unknown sphere of the supersensible than any kind of thought could do.[5] The good will surpasses all understanding; in this way the

5. See, for example, L. W. Beck (trans.), *Critique of Practical Reason* (Chicago: University of Chicago Press, 1949), p. 248.

word of the Gospel is transformed by the Kantian spirit. The moral imperative is not only a sure guide in life, but if we follow it we shall be transported beyond the limits of our existence or beyond the limit of that world which we can perceive and know through science. Thus within our will a light is kindled which illuminates another world, the world of absolute values, as a modern philosopher might say. If we subject ourselves to the moral imperative voluntarily, not in subservient obedience, but in the way in which the scientist subjects his will to the imperative of truth, then our practical will is ennobled, just as our theoretical will is ennobled by following the guiding star of truth. Kant is in complete agreement with Lessing. He is convinced that it is more worthwhile and worthy to strive for truth than to possess it, or as Lessing puts it, "If God held all truth sealed in his right hand, and all striving after truth (with the provision that I would eternally err) in his left, and said to me, 'Choose!' I would humbly point to the left hand and say, 'Father, give me that one, because pure truth is for you alone.' "[6]

The idea that man through the moral imperative is in harmony with a higher world, that moral action liberates him from natural necessity, determines Kant's

6. *Eine Duplik,* 1778, *Sämmtliche Werke,* ed. Lachmann (1839), X, 49–50.

Weltanschauung even more decisively. Behind this idea looms the further thought that the moral certainty concerning the existence of a supersensible world directly forbids us to go beyond it and demand knowledge of the supersensible. We are not only forever unable to possess such knowledge, we should not even covet it. For, as Kant says, "We know nothing of the future, and we ought not to seek to know more than what is rationally bound up with the incentives of morality and their end."[7]

If our ignorance were simply derived from the inability to know what we want to know, Kant's voluntarism would only be the outcome of an intellectualistic resignation, a kind of philosophical subterfuge, a miserable substitute for the truth not accessible to man. It is in keeping with the spirit of Kant's philosophy to interpret it as a doctrine which bases our metaphysical ignorance on an ethical injunction prohibiting us to know theoretically metaphysical truth. In this interpretation Kant's primacy of the practical reason reaches its consummation.

For Kant moral obligation is something ultimate and absolute; it signifies the limit and also the summit of all human consciousness. In fact, it signifies the peak

7. Theodore M. Greene and Hoyt H. Hudson (trans.), *Religion within the Limits of Reason Alone* (Chicago: Open Court Publishing Co., 1934), p. 149, n.

23

of man's whole existence. To explain it or to derive it from a higher source would only deprive this obligation of its unrelieved gravity and its inexorable rigor. He who is bold enough to presume that it is possible to transcend the limit of the moral consciousness, and to throw off the bonds which constrain us as moral beings, violates the eternal law and makes himself a companion of the gods or of the devil in order to escape the burden of duty. Not only does such a transgression run counter to the finitude of our intellect but, what is of greater moment, our moral conscience is opposed to it as well. We ought not to exercise our curiosity over any question that would surpass our ethical horizon. Morality is meaningful only as long as we are imperfect, i.e., as long as we strive. A metaphysical knowledge which in theory would do away with our imperfection would necessarily endanger the majesty of the moral law; it would enrich our theoretical knowledge at the expense of our moral will. We are under the moral law and should never place ourselves above it, as metaphysical knowledge would do. We ought to overcome our imperfection instead of justifying it, as a metaphysic seeking to explain the world must attempt to do.

In order to understand the deep roots of Kant's moral Weltanschauung, we must bear in mind the

words of Goethe: *"Es irrt der Mensch, solang er strebt."*
One could render this in the spirit of Kant as: "Man
strives only as long as he errs." If man ceases to err, he
ceases to strive; he who pretends to absolute truth
would surely relax in the unending moral struggle.
Failing this, he would become indifferent to whether
the world is essentially good and divine or whether it
simply has no regard for moral and religious values.
We have an excellent example of such a process in
Schopenhauer's quietism. If, as Schopenhauer thought,
the ultimate ground of existence is devoid of any rationality and is nothing but a blind impulse, who, under these conditions, would any longer be interested in
the struggle of life? Who in such a world would pursue ideal ends and carry them through conscientiously?
A man would try to do away with all moral commit-
ments and indeed with the will itself; the voice of his
illusory metaphysical knowledge would drown out the
voice of his conscience and he would rather rely on his
speculative certainty than submit to the commandment
of the moral law.

It is no accident that Schopenhauer speaks about the
blessed calm of nothingness which he prefers to the
will. But even an optimistic metaphysics finally ends
in making the state of intellectual satisfaction superior
to the untiring impulse of insatiable striving, for all

metaphysics looks down upon everything human as something that is not absolute and is even superseded by the absolute. Moral consciousness cannot be the absolute to the man who believes that he has penetrated into the core of all things; however, unless morality is ultimate its very nature and existence is denied for, according to Kant, it is the essence of the moral to be the ultimate. If, on the other hand, morality is an ultimate, then we must conclude that all speculative knowledge cannot be ultimate, for knowledge of any kind is subordinate to the moral law.

A more extreme anti-intellectualism is hard to conceive. Kant boldly deduces the moral necessity of assuming that the world is finally incomprehensible from the unconditioned validity of the moral "ought." If, like Spinoza or Leibniz, we fancy that we are able to know in what sense God dictated his laws to the world, then we could not take account of the testimony of moral consciousness in our attempt to comprehend the ultimate scheme of things. Even though metaphysical systems may try to reserve a place for moral action in the world as they view it, their Weltanschauung precludes the truly moral spirit. The commandment of reason to subdue passions and inclinations becomes meaningless if the sequence of occurrences is ordered once and for all. If a divine substance is the essence of all things, if God's intellect and will so govern the world that our own consciousness is nothing but the incidental occasion for the display of divine power, then only one thing would really make sense, i.e., to contemplate this display and to comprehend its order theoretically.

Every metaphysical system conceives of the world as something finished and thereby leaves the will with nothing to do. Hence it was consistent when Spinoza like Aristotle said that the contemplation of the idea of God is the highest virtue and when he called his metaphysics, i.e., the scientific knowledge of the eternal substance, ethics. He who takes his metaphysics to be the truth will not continue to strive any more than would the disciple of Schopenhauer; instead he will believe that he has overcome the world and that he can be content with intellectual love of God. Kant therefore held that such a metaphysic is not only an intellectual blind alley but also an aberration of moral reason, because a metaphysical system produces an illusory knowledge which shakes man's moral foundation and violates the majesty of the moral "ought." According to the view of the metaphysical thinkers, only he who agrees with their systems is virtuous. Kant, on the contrary, agrees with the common man that virtue can be possessed by the unlearned no less than by the learned; his philosophy is the most emphatic protest against the view which would ascribe virtue only to a privileged class of men, such as philosophers or sages. Virtue is not knowledge; what is given to science will have to be taken from "con-science."[8]

From the foregoing it can be seen how closely Kant's doctrine of the limits of knowledge is connected with the spirit of his entire Weltanschauung. Amid the uncertainty and insecurity of earthly life the moral law stands as our only trustworthy guide. Our ignorance about metaphysical truth is as inescapable theoretically as it is necessary morally. It is implied in the very ideal of the "ought" as the unconditional imperative that, whatever may be the origin of the moral law, beings who are subject to it must be theoretically and practically imperfect, ever unfinished, ever on their way toward a distant goal. They are forever striving and being striven against, they are forever victors and vanquished. Beatific vision is granted to us only in aesthetic joy; it is denied us in the moral realm and therefore also denied in philosophical knowledge.

8. The German text has a fine parallelism here, "was dem *Wissen* gegeben wird, das wird dem Gewissen genommen werden müssen," which I am attempting to preserve in English by using the words "science" and "con-science." It is true, however, that "Wissen" would be more properly translated by the word "knowledge" as in the first part of the sentence.

Artistic pleasure itself does not interfere with the significance of moral life because the two are not in conflict. Only an aesthetic Weltanschauung, that is, an aesthetic intuition expanded into a cosmic intuition, would conflict with the moral ought. Such an aesthetic intuition which results in an aesthetic metaphysics is regarded by Kant as both fallacious and misleading, like every mystical intuition which presumes to overcome our moral imperfection and thereby seduces us into believing in a metaphysics. The moral consciousness alone should determine our Weltanschauung. The ethical Weltanschauung, however, can never become metaphysics; indeed, in a literal sense it can never become an ethical "world intuition," since the world as a whole can never be understood from the standpoint of ethics.

Fichte was the first to misinterpret (perhaps deliberately) Kant's philosophy by means of such a metaphysics. According to Kant, ethics replaces metaphysics. Kant's view is poles apart from the view that the world can be comprehended in a moral way; on the contrary, he insists that morality makes the world incomprehensible.

II

Ethical Dualism

THE problem of a monistic world system belongs among the most significant philosophical problems of all time. Therefore it will be of interest to ask whether Kant can be classified as a monistic thinker or not. What is frequently understood by monism in modern times is something rather superficial. Modern philosophy rarely recognizes the true duality which must be transformed into unity. It regards the contrast of the physical and the psychical as the highest contrast and therefore strives for a union of the two, i.e., for a psycho-physical substance or energy which would enable us to comprehend the world as a whole. But the world is not fully embraced simply by distinguishing and uniting body and soul, or nature and mind. The contrast which is deeper by far and which is made central by Kant is the contrast between nature and morality, between what is and what ought to be, or between necessity and freedom.

Kant is a monistic thinker in so far as his philosophy leads to a faith in an ultimate unity of these separate realms, a unity in which nature is subordinated to moral ends. Such a unity is postulated by moral reason. Kant is, however, a dualist in so far as he denies the possibility of any theoretical knowledge of this unity. Thus we meet a conflict of motives operative in Kant's Weltanschauung; this conflict of monistic and dualistic tendencies and claims touches upon the deepest problems of his, and indeed of all, philosophy.

In so far as Kant regards the categorical imperative as an ultimate principle he is forced to retain the dualism of inclination and duty, of desire and will, and finally the duality of nature and freedom. Nevertheless the emphasis placed upon moral life leads him, paradoxically enough, to postulate a higher unity of the two realms. Moral decision and action would lose all their meaning if they took place in a world completely alien to them; or if moral intention had no relation whatever to an objective order transcending it; or if we were not able to believe that the human will is supported by a divine will. What renders moral activity metaphysically significant is precisely Kant's conviction that the supersensible speaks through morality; it is Kant's contention that the moral realm points to the ultimate ground of all being and all existence.

From this it follows that the moral law leads to something which transcends both the necessity of nature and even the normative character of the imperative itself. In the last analysis it postulates an ascendancy over existence; it points to a transcendent One which would ultimately unite the realm of nature and the realm of morality. The metaphysical quality of the moral law is not merely its moral quality. The moral law not only commands man to subject both his own nature and external nature to reason, but it postulates the confidence that such subjection is possible, that neither our natural impressions and desires nor the outer world of sense present insurmountable obstacles to our obedience to its moral command. This confidence or faith presupposes an original harmony between what is and what we ought to do. It presupposes an order which is neither that of nature alone nor that of moral norms but one which guarantees that the moral commands can be carried through in the world in which we live.

If we would understand this idea in a more concrete way, we must note the fact that in Kant's Weltanschauung man is a point in which the two different world spheres of nature and morality meet. Man is a biological organism developed from the brutes, yet he is also much more than an animal. This temporally and spatially insignificant natural creature is, nevertheless, a citizen of the supersensible world; man is able by the power of his moral reason to establish for both himself and his actions a value which transcends all time and all space and puts him in touch with an eternal being. This overwhelming relationship permeates Kant's thought throughout; it prompts him to assume a supersensible ground of nature and morality and leads him to postulate some ultimate subject as the author and sustainer of man in his dual status.

The difficulty of uniting necessity and freedom always reveals itself when we confront an ultimate monism. If we forget that this problem cannot be solved except on the basis of man's moral life, we might be tempted to think of nature as the ultimate monistic ground of all existence, but then this would mean that we reduce moral motivations to biological instincts or organic desires. Or it would mean that we interpret nature in a metaphysical fashion, thereby running the risk of losing both the clarity of the concept of nature and the precision of morality. All the categories which are peculiar to the sphere of moral life, categories like freedom, duty, conscience, motive, guilt, responsibility, etc., would then either be ignored or distorted. As compared with such a vague monism which supposes that one and the same thing is thought whenever the same word is used, Kant's position recommends itself because of its great clarity. He always emphasizes differences without in the least obscuring them, but he also recognizes the unavoidable task of relating them to each other in a harmonious system. In the end he envisages the solution of this problem as one which in spite of its inescapable character can never be attained.

The solution must be found because the idea of an all-embracing unity is legitimate. A reason must be given why the moral law is ordained for man as a sensible being although it is addressed to him as a rational being. If the task which has to be performed were merely theoretical, there would be no necessary ground for preferring either nature or the moral realm as representing the unity of both. It is for moral reasons that nature cannot be regarded as constituting both itself and the realm of morality, but neither, on the other hand, can the moral law be the ground of its unity with nature. However, Kant seeks for the highest synthesis not merely on theoretical but on primarily ethical grounds. The spirit of his Weltanschauung demands a moral world order as a postulate of moral reason. But it must not be obscured that Kant's attempt to solve this problem is not altogether free from ambiguities. It is these ambiguities that prompted his successors to transform his philosophy in a number of ways.

Two motives not easily combined and in competition with each other determine Kant's doctrine at this point: an ethical and a religious motive. On the one hand, Kant is deeply convinced that all religious life must result from a moral disposition of mind, or even more that religious life is nothing but a special mode of moral life; on the other hand, he feels himself compelled to declare that God is higher even than the moral law. Thus a conflict of motives results which eventually threatens his Weltanschauung with an inner contradiction. I will first describe in detail the ethical motive in so far as it tends to triumph over the religious one.

Seen from the standpoint of this motive one can say, without fear of exaggeration, that in Kant's Weltanschauung the moral law takes the place of God. God is, as Fichte ventured to put it later on, the *ordo ordinans,* i.e., the ordering order which is actualized in our moral action. God is the moral imperative; his will expresses itself in the voice of our conscience, his curse in remorse, and his love in the blessed happiness of a pure heart. According to this view, there is no other service of God, no other glorification of God, but obedience to the moral law.[1] Kant has often been called the philos-

1. L. W. Beck (trans.), *Critique of Practical Reason* (Chicago: University of Chicago Press, 1949), p. 234; cf. *Bestimmung des Begriffs einer Menschenrasse* (1785), *Gesammelte Schriften* (Akademie Ausg.), VIII, 104.

opher of Protestantism; this is true if one takes seriously the emphasis he put on conscience as the highest tribunal of the moral and religious consciousness. In this respect the Kantian philosophy differs most from that of Thomism. The subjectivism which is here implied in Kant's Weltanschauung will be discussed later on. At this juncture I shall call attention only to the primacy of the moral consciousness, a primacy which holds even within the sphere of religion itself.

It cannot be denied that here there is a certain proud independence which reveals a kinship with the sentiments of the young Goethe as expressed in his poem "Prometheus."[2] This feeling of human independence is most clearly revealed in the idea of autonomy, in the idea that not God but we ourselves, in so far as we embody pure practical reason, are the legislators of the moral law. We submit to the law not on God's behalf but for our own sake. It is our true will that must be done.

The moral freedom of man is thus not merely a freedom from nature, but also a freedom from external supernatural powers. No one before Kant had ever exalted man so much; no one had ever accorded him such a degree of metaphysical independence and self-

2. E. A. Bowring *et al.* (trans.), *The Poems of Goethe* (Cambridge ed.; Boston, 1882).

dependence. Within himself man creates and preserves the supersensible as that excellence which distinguishes him from all other beings. The supersensible is precisely that trait which makes man what he is or rather what he ought to be. The idea of mankind and the idea of God are indeed so near to each other here that they almost coincide. Even God is dependent upon the moral law instead of the law being dependent upon him.

But what place still remains in the world for a God who is so circumscribed? What kind of dignity, what kind of majesty can still be attributed to him? Is God so conceived anything more than an ideal of mankind? Is he anything more than a postulate which agrees with our moral need, as Kant puts it,[3] but which nevertheless remains problematic? A contemporary thinker[4]

3. Beck, *op. cit.*, p. 228.

4. Kroner is referring here to Hans Vaihinger (1852–1933), a member of the group of neo-Kantians who were engaged in repudiating the metaphysical systems of Fichte, Schelling, and Hegel in order to get "back to Kant" and to primarily epistemological questions. Vaihinger's thought is distinguished from that of his colleagues in the movement by its positivistic bent. In a book well known in English, *The Philosophy of "As If"* (Eng. trans. of *Philosophie des Als Ob,* 1911), Vaihinger developed the thesis that all domains of thought, science as well as religion, are dependent upon mental fictions which are both necessary and at the same time incapable of being defended as parts of knowledge. Those who interpret Kant as holding that we must act "as if" God exists (imply-

believed himself in agreement with Kant's view when he interpreted it as meaning that we ought to act *as if* God existed, and nothing more. Kant never used exactly these words but at times he expresses himself in a way which lends support to such an interpretation. What then is the right interpretation? Are not they on the right track who suggest that Kant was not absolutely in earnest when he propounded faith in God?[5] Did Kant perhaps merely say that faith is a moral need and a moral idea, but that nothing can finally be decided concerning the question whether God really exists or not?

Such an interpretation would indeed be in harmony with the assertion that the moral law is fundamentally Kant's God and that there is no God beyond it.

Such an interpretation cannot be maintained.[6] A man of the intellectual and moral stature of Kant seriously means what he says; all of his words and writings testify to a character of extraordinary moral

---

ing either that God does not exist or that we know absolutely nothing about such a conclusion) have usually arrived at their view through the influence of Vaihinger's ideas.

5. For example, even such a dependable scholar as J. E. Erdmann in his *Versuch einer wissenschaftlichen Darstellung der neueren Philosophie* (1848), III, 177, supports such a view.

6. Heinrich Rickert, *Fichtes Atheismusstreit und die Kantische Philosophie* (1899).

earnestness. Moreover, such an interpretation runs counter to Kant's whole Weltanschauung. Faith in a supersensible unity of nature and freedom is a necessary consequence of Kant's entire system. Faith in the existence of God springs from the very foundation of his thought and is an indispensable element within it. When Kant says that it is morally necessary to believe in God he does not say that it is questionable whether God really exists; rather, he insists that the existence of God, though it cannot be demonstrated by theoretical reason, nevertheless is assured on moral grounds. Within the confines of Kant's Weltanschauung no stronger argument could have been given.

To be morally necessary implies for Kant that God's existence is even more firmly established than it would be if it rested upon speculative arguments; for the moral law is on a par with the laws of nature with respect to certainty but surpasses them with respect to dignity of content. Theoretical reasons can be refuted; if God is proved he is also exposed to doubt, for theories and inferences may easily be erroneous. If God's existence is morally postulated it is irrefutable; it could be denied only if the validity of the moral law were denied, but that for Kant would mean that man should deny that he is man. If faith in God is a postulate of moral reason, his existence is as unshakably certain as is the validity of the moral law itself: this is Kant's authentic conviction.

The morally postulated God exists just as surely as we ourselves exist as moral beings; after all, even our own existence cannot be theoretically demonstrated but is itself morally postulated. The same radical, almost religious, conviction which underlies Kant's doctrine of the moral law also underlies his doctrine of God's existence. Any doubt cast upon the second doctrine must necessarily affect the validity of the first. Consequently, the thesis which maintains that there is an unexpressed disbelief implied in the demand that we should always act as if God existed, not only misconceives Kant's religious attitude, but also nullifies the ethical content and even the theoretical outcome of his Weltanschauung.

In mentioning the inner ambiguity of Kant's Weltanschauung, I did not mean to imply the absence of belief in God, as some misguided Kantians have erroneously suggested. What I wished to emphasize was, not the absence of honest conviction on Kant's part, but rather the fact that within that conviction a conflict exists between contrasting motifs. This conflict might be understood as arising out of the rivalry between Kant's ethical voluntarism and his religious faith. Although Kant's doctrine of a postulated faith and a postulated God seems to be a logical consequence of his ethical views, it is true nevertheless that such moral and rational faith is not wholly consistent with the moral foundation of his Weltanschauung. According to the ethical motif, the moral law is an absolute and an ultimate; according to the doctrine of the postulate, the moral law is neither the absolute nor the ultimate, and it is this incongruity which disturbs the whole argument. Obviously Kant is oscillating between an ethical and a religious Weltanschauung without arriving at any definitive and satisfying resolution of the conflict.[7] From the religious point of view (which may at the same time be called a metaphysical tendency within the critical system), it is not legitimate for Kant to allow the moral motif to triumph; rather he must look for a transcendent unity embracing the realms of nature and morality, of necessity and freedom. The moral law is the ultimate for us, while that unity is the ultimate in itself (the "thing-in-itself").

Since Kant as a critical thinker excludes any comprehension of the ultimate as it is in itself except through the mediation of the ultimate as it is for us, he is compelled to derive whatever knowledge of God may be possible within his system from the moral law. Thus

7. The same point can be seen in Kant's *Religion within the Limits of Reason Alone,* trans. T. M. Greene and H. H. Hudson (Chicago: Open Court Publishing Co., 1934).

two conflicting tendencies collide in Kant's conception of God; the supreme being, on the one hand, has to be morally postulated, and faith in him is to be vindicated on moral grounds alone, while on the other hand, Kant realizes that God is the absolutely sovereign and supreme being, beyond and above all relations, to be vindicated by nothing but himself. The tremendous height to which man is raised by Kant through the idea of moral autonomy and freedom necessarily makes it difficult to transcend ethics. The metaphysical significance which Kant attributes to the moral will, and which forms the very center of his ethical voluntarism, inevitably detracts somewhat from his doctrine of faith. The God of faith appears as a God whose majesty is dependent on the majesty of the moral law. Kant was certainly the first thinker in the history of philosophy to assert and defend the full autonomy and self-sufficiency of the ethical will, but in so doing it appears that he did not do full justice to the religious life of the soul. He shattered philosophical intellectualism, but he fell, at the same time, into a philosophical "ethicism." This ethicism was as much a stumbling block to a full recognition of religious life as intellectualism had been an impediment to moral life.

However, even the ethical principle somewhat suffers from Kant's doctrine of a postulated faith.

Through this doctrine the idea of God tends to lose its majesty and sovereignty, just as the idea of the moral law in turn runs the risk of losing its clear and forthright meaning. Kant introduced moral faith in order to guarantee that moral action has moral consequences in a world of sense which is morally indifferent. Reason, he argues, postulates a divine order of the world for the purpose of binding together the spheres of what is real and what ought to be real. But is such a theory possible for Kant and is he consistent? Does not the autonomy and sovereignty of the moral law rest precisely on the contrast between morality and nature, between the "is" and the "ought"? Is not just this the essence of duty, according to Kant, that duty is opposed to the impulses and inclinations of nature? If the opposition between the two is mitigated, if we concede that there is a secret unity of the natural and moral realms, then, so it seems, the seriousness of the imperative is endangered. The very struggle of moral life, without which moral life is unthinkable, would then cease to exist. The ethical Weltanschauung inexorably demands an enduring tension betwen the will and its goal; the moral will loses its true power if this obstacle is eliminated. The moral law itself loses its meaning if the tension and the obstacle are removed.

How can we reconcile the absolute sovereignty, the

metaphysical ultimacy, of the moral law with the doctrine that this law is restricted in its validity to the sphere of human life? How can we believe that we are obliged to lead a life filled with exertion and struggle against impulses and inclinations and yet also believe that this struggle at bottom is no struggle at all, that instinct and imperative are not ultimately antagonistic to each other? How can we believe that we are subject to one master who commands the two opposed spheres and moreover does so for moral purposes? Does this not imply that man as a moral being ought to live as if God did not exist or, as Kant says, "as though everything depended on him (man),"[8] whereas man as a religious being should live as if God did exist? Does this not also imply that we ought to believe that we must work for the coming of the divine kingdom without any reliance upon an outward power which would help us, and yet that we also should believe that without the aid of God his Kingdom can never come? Does this not finally mean that whether God exists or not, the moral law loses its meaning? If God exists, the struggle is pointless and the power of the "ought" collapses; if God does not exist, the struggle is purposeless and the moral law becomes a mad tyrant which reason can no longer acknowledge.

8. *Ibid.*, p. 92.

In the end the moral Weltanschauung is weakened by the religious postulates which, according to Kant, are its necessary correlates. In the one case God, postulated by the moral will, is not accorded his divine right; while in the other case the moral life severed from God is in danger of losing its moral meaning at the moment God is postulated. God as well as the moral law becomes ambivalent; they appear at the same time to be both independent and dependent upon each other, absolute and yet non-absolute. The moral certainty that God exists finally leads us to a position not so different from that taken by metaphysical knowledge; both sap the strength needed for the campaign against sensuality and desire, the campaign against evil.

Kant once said that God in his wisdom has arranged matters so that we cannot prove his existence theoretically. Could we prove it, we no longer would act from the sense of duty but from fear.[9] Should we not rather conclude that he who was certain of God's existence would not act at all, because he would then have only one desire left, namely, to contemplate the glory of God? However this may be, Kant admits that the certainty of God's existence seems to be more a hindrance than a help to the moral life. But is this certainty of a

9. Beck, *op. cit.,* pp. 246–47.

moral faith different from that of a metaphysical knowledge? This, as I have shown, cannot be Kant's opinion.

The ambiguity of Kant's ethical Weltanschauung thus stands out clearly. Kant intends to exalt the moral law as the summit of man's total existence, and yet he also wants to put God above this summit. He cannot truly reconcile these two motifs. He can neither render to God his full sovereignty nor can he attribute to the moral law what he would like to attribute to it. It is precisely this ambiguity which prompted Kant's successors to reconstruct and thereby to demolish his philosophical edifice. But, unfortunately, they also failed to throw light on the darkness of this profound and puzzling problem. Perhaps this is because we finally encounter an eternal antinomy which even the ingenuity of Kant could neither evade nor solve, although he struggled to dispense with metaphysics just because he recognized the inevitability of such an antinomy.

If we continue to grope for reasons for this contradiction or discord within the Kantian Weltanschauung, we discover that they are inextricably tied to the very foundations of his ethical voluntarism. The idea of the imperative inexorably impels us to go beyond its confines. It is precisely from the standpoint of moral life that it is impossible to desire the perpetuation of the contrast between inclination and duty, nature and freedom. It is the final elimination of this contrast which should be considered the ultimate goal. The moral will ought to strive for the attainment of an absolutely moral state and this implies that such a will must strive for its own destruction. The moral imperative therefore cannot be thought of as an ultimate in the way Kant's ethical Weltanschauung requires.[10]

The voluntarist who finds the metaphysical in the moral will itself is thereby driven to abandon his own position and finally to gain the insight that the voluntaristic view itself cannot be absolute. It seems that a Weltanschauung which refuses to take an absolute position cannot be a Weltanschauung at all, since the very meaning and function of Weltanschauung is to view existence from an absolute standpoint. If the ethical Weltanschauung cannot be ultimate, then it is for this very reason not Weltanschauung at all. Moral life, in spite of its exalted character, is not altogether appropriate for interpreting the totality of existence; for the sake of such interpretation it is necessary to

10. Kroner's discussion of the implications of Kant's moral theory should be compared with Hegel's critical analysis of Kant in the section "Morality" to be found in his *Phenomenology*. See J. B. Baillie (trans.), *The Phenomenology of Mind* (London: Allen & Unwin, 1931), pp. 611–79.

adopt a standpoint which transcends the moral horizon. It is, however, neither my intention nor my task in this essay to consider the possibilities which might lead to a new approach to these ultimate problems.

How does Kant himself try to overcome the difficulties which, as we have seen, arise in his picture of the world? The difficulties all originate from the same source. We human beings, according to Kant, find ourselves limited and finite, whereas the Weltanschauung at which we aim is necessarily bound to surpass those limitations and confinements. We can never completely succeed in surpassing them, we can only strive for completion. Therefore we fall victim to a contradiction: Weltanschauung demands the completion of our striving, while our humanity prevents us from attaining it. As finite beings we can never reach wisdom; the highest thing we can accomplish is love of wisdom, i.e., philo-sophy. If finite and limited beings seek the infinite and unlimited, the result can only be that the infinite and unlimited will be forced into a finite and limited mold.

In this way we can clarify the ultimate contradictions within the Kantian philosophy and the obscurity of his Weltanschauung. The contradictions are not the result of Kant's personal shortcomings, rather they follow directly from his premises. Kant teaches that we as human beings can only grasp the ultimate from our own position, and therefore only as an unattainable ideal, and not as a truth within our reach. The ethical premise requires that the goal be beyond our action, for should the goal be one which we could actually reach it would be no goal at all, and thus it could no longer be conceived in an ethical way; it would be something completely beyond our horizons. Only what is not realizable can be ethically commanded, a command which can be absolutely fulfilled is no longer ultimate. Thus we conclude that Kant believes in a limitation of knowledge based on an ethical command. Even faith, in so far as it springs from the moral will, cannot change this basic insight. Faith, although it is not distinguished from knowledge with respect to its certainty, yet differs from it in that its content does not need to conform to the logical law of contradiction. It is just this difference which distinguishes faith from a philosophical system. Faith is unconcerned about the contradiction involved in its being ultimate, yet only ultimate within the horizon of man.

In Kant's philosophy the access to the ultimate as the content of faith is, however, an ethical one and, to this extent, a rational one. Faith itself, therefore, is also rational, and this in a sense doubles the contradiction and makes it less tolerable, because faith, being rational, leads us to expect a logically consistent resolution which is not forthcoming. Kant's God should be conceived as in agreement with the law of contradiction; a contradiction in the content of a rational faith offends reason. We cannot rationally believe in a God who is logically inconsistent, for the very idea of God demands that he is beyond all imperfections, even beyond those which are connected with the mode of belief. Within the scope of the Kantian Weltanschauung it is impossible that faith should be separated from its source in the moral will, and it is just on this account that faith cannot lay claim to interpret the world from a vantage point higher than that of ethics. The intrinsic ambiguity of the voluntaristic Weltanschauung consequently cannot be avoided or overcome by the founding of a moral religion.

So far as Kant is able to vindicate religious faith at all, such faith is completely dependent on the sphere of the moral reason which postulates it. In the last analysis Kant not only proclaims the primacy of practical over theoretical reason but—and this is even more decisive for his Weltanschauung—he proclaims the primacy of the moral over the religious consciousness as well. Moral life can give faith its content but faith can never give to moral life its content. Faith can never provide a basis for the autonomy of the moral will; rather, it is the moral law which provides a basis for faith. Moreover, God can be interpreted from the standpoint of human striving while this striving can never be interpreted from God's vantage point.

If, therefore, we take the word "Weltanschauung" literally, we arrive at the truly Kantian conclusion that we can never arrive at any Weltanschauung which is free from contradiction; what is ultimate in itself will ever remain what is ultimate for us, and therefore every Weltanschauung will inevitably encounter contradictions. What we can attain at best without contradicting ourselves is an intuition not of the world but only of our own life, and this is precisely the meaning of the expression "ethical Weltanschauung." Such a Weltanschauung is basically a vision of life or a doctrine about the meaning of man.

This meaning demands moral consummation of myself and of all other personalities, in other words, it concerns the approach to a kingdom of heaven on earth. Faith in God supports and encourages the moral will in its arduous task. However, this support should never be allowed to diminish our obligation to work and struggle for the goal; on the contrary, God only helps him who merits such help through his own effort and action. Moral intentions vindicate faith in the reality of such divine assistance. From the point of view of morality submission to the moral law is clearly compatible with faith, whereas it would be immoral to infer from the existence of the Almighty that the moral law is void and man's exertion superfluous. We should never ask how a divine world government is logically possible, or how such a government can be reconciled to the fact of evil which Kant holds to be radical, or even how such a government can leave room for a moral law. Such questions aspire to something that surpasses our capacity; they aspire to knowledge of the absolute. Faith is precisely that certainty which can be maintained by the moral will. This is the best definition which is in accord with Kant.

The content of faith transcends reason. It is just as impossible to derive this content from logical principles as to derive the content of the will from logical principles. Although Kant would not agree with Tertullian's *credo quia absurdum,* yet he would be inclined to say: I believe although I cannot comprehend; I believe, not in order to comprehend (as Augustine says), not in order to acquire cognitive certainty by means of faith, but rather in order to support the will. Knowledge in Augustine's sense would merely achieve a too easy compromise between faith and reason, whereas true faith points to the superrational as well as to the supersensible. Kant rejects all attempts at such a compromise.

The incomprehensibility of the Divine does not mean something merely negative; it is not simply a resignation of the intellect. Instead Kant wishes to replace metaphysics and its intellectual claims by the will and the rational faith which is grounded on it. However, with such a basis faith is nothing but the functionary of the will. The incomprehensible becomes in its positive significance the goal of striving; the content of faith performs the function of assuring us that this goal can be reached. It is in this sense that the famous words, "I felt obliged to deny knowledge in order to make room for faith," should be interpreted. In accord with the spirit of Kant's Weltanschauung we can assert that faith takes the place of metaphysical knowledge, because Kant's metaphysics is thoroughly voluntaristic and dualistic. Kant denies knowledge not primarily for the sake of faith but in order to make room for the will. Not faith, but the life of the will is the focal point of Kant's Weltanschauung.

Only now can we fully understand how completely the term voluntarism is justified as a characterization of the ultimate intention of the Kantian philosophy. Kant is so far from countenancing any form of intellectualism that he proves the moral necessity of faith although this faith logically contradicts itself.[11] Facing the ultimate questions man can only take a moral, not a rational, position. What indeed could be a better indication of Kant's anti-intellectualism? For the way in which a thinker tries to answer the ultimate questions reveals his standpoint more clearly than does any detail of his system.

Only now can we fully appreciate in what sense Kant's philosophy is dualistic and in what sense it is monistic. The unity of the two separate realms of nature and freedom is an object not of knowledge but of faith alone. A monistic philosophy is therefore impossible. We shall never be able to understand how the same being, namely man, can at the same time be a creature of nature and yet participate in a supernatural moral order. Nor can we understand what kind of "sameness" conjoins the opposite spheres apart from the moral consciousness which commands us to obey its law in the midst of an indifferent or resisting nature. We shall never be able to conceive the reason of this duality from a monistic point of view.

Man's moral consciousness demands that he believes in an ultimate unity of the spheres (otherwise he could not even act, much less hope that moral actions would have moral consequences), but his Weltanschauung

11. Beck, *op. cit.*, pp. 322–23, n.

must be rooted in the dualism of the spheres. Only where the separation of nature and freedom exists can he find any meaning in moral effort and action, and only where he finds this meaning does the very word Weltanschauung become meaningful. The world has meaning according to Kant only on the presupposition that human actions are meaningful. "Meaning of the world" is not a theoretical but a practical concept. The philosophical dualism is therefore the precondition of the very question concerning the ultimate meaning of existence.

In a world interpreted monistically norms as well as ends, rules as well as purposes, would be meaningless. Consequently such a world would itself be devoid of meaning; it could never satisfy the human longing for meaning. Such a world could not even give a clue as to the riddle of why we puzzle about ourselves or how beings like ourselves are possible at all. Such a world therefore could never give rise to any philosophy whatsoever. If this is true, then the world can be meaningful only if it is meaningful to us, only if it is so organized that the life of our will is meaningful. And thus an original duality must exist as a moral necessity. Only the duality of beginning and end, of a point from which the will departs and a point toward which it strives; only the duality of what is and what ought to be, the duality of the real and the ideal, is in conformity with the moral consciousness.

But just as the idea of what ought to be constantly points beyond itself (because every achievement calls forth new duties and tasks), so the idea of an absolute meaning also leads beyond itself. We must admit that there cannot be any meaning at all beyond that of purpose and end, and that meaning implies purpose (if it is not actually identical with it). Nevertheless, we are led to assume that there is an end beyond all ends, a purpose beyond all purposes—an absolute meaning beyond all relative and finite meanings. All human striving postulates such a definitive and ultimate goal, for as human it is forever incomplete and as striving it always posits a meaning beyond itself—an absolute meaning implying an absolute fulfilment, and thus an absolute unity transcending the duality which characterizes our human situation. However, we have no concept of such a unity. We find ourselves unable to understand what absolute fulfilment means in concrete terms, or what end it is which has no longer to be willed because it is forever realized. Beyond the duality of beginning and end, beyond the tension of the real and the ideal and consequently of good and evil, all meaning seems to disappear. We cannot want such a meaning to exist, because it would destroy the meaning of our own life. Kant quotes with approval the words of the poet Haller:[12]

> The world with all its faults
> Is better than a realm of will-less angels.

Kant's vision of life thus demands an ethical dualism. Within ourselves there is a capacity for rising above the level of nature, above the level of this earthly world, and indeed above even the cosmos itself. The moral will soars above the confines of time and space into the supersensible and it acquires an eternal value by subjecting itself to the moral law. In a world which, without freedom and without consciousness, blindly obeys mathematical laws, in a world of organic beings who are slaves of their impulses and desires and who are subject to and determined by the end of self-preservation, man stands as lawgiver and sovereign. For man stamps upon things the seal of his freedom and by establishing state and church he creates norms and patterns of moral community. Thus he founds within the scope of the world of sense a supersensible order and gradually brings the Kingdom of God into existence.

In contrast to this philosophical pride which exalts man, a much more modest view is also to be found in Kant. The ethical greatness of man is counterbalanced

12. Greene and Hudson, *op. cit.,* p. 58. The original is in Albrecht von Haller, *Über den Ursprung des Übels* (1734).

by his ethical weakness and corruption, the metaphysical horizon is limited by the physical roots of man's existence. There is radical evil in every human being which revolts against the legislation of the moral consciousness and persuades man to regard moral reason as an invidious tyrant from which he should try to escape. Kant denies that the contest between the good and the evil incentives in man, whether in the individual or in society, in private or in public life, can ever end. Man will always be divided into a lord and a bondsman or slave. If he makes his inclinations the maxim of his decisions and actions, the moral law transforms itself into an inexorable judge which condemns and punishes. Kant is a moral pessimist. We are not born to find peace and rest in any state of the soul, rather the law is an ever present goal spurring the will on toward the good, though impulses and inclinations continually tempt us in the direction of evil.

Kant's Weltanschauung therefore does not favor the attempt later made by Fichte to lead man to béatitude. Kant leaves no doubt that he does not believe in the possibility (or even the moral value) of a beatific state of mind. Man is eternally imperfect, he is forever (even beyond the grave) in the making, never reaching his goal, always divided against himself. The deification of the soul which the mystics describe is to Kant a product of a vain enthusiasm which produces in us the illusion that we are endowed with a capacity which we do not in fact possess. Kant explicitly denies that any man can have an intimate intercourse with God, such as the self-styled "favorite of heaven"[13] claims to enjoy. The claim of mystical certainty and of mystical union with God militates no less surely against our moral undertaking than does the overambitious claim to metaphysical knowledge.

We are driven from paradise, and the assiduous fulfilment of our duties alone can point the way toward the heavenly goal. Thus the Kantian God is enthroned in awesome majesty and, in relation to us, stands at an unapproachable distance. The divine love cannot be acquired and enjoyed like a piece of property; it can only be the remote fruit of that worship of God which is synonymous with moral conduct and which is in most cases hard and trying. Although Kant endeavors to adjust the Christian idea of the forgiving and redeeming God to his moral Weltanschauung, it cannot be denied that the God of wrath and vengeance is more in accord with his outlook. This Weltanschauung does not veil or mitigate the dreadful fact that in God's world evil exists and that the good man no less than the wicked must suffer. It is this fact above all which makes our existence, as well as the existence and the very nature of God, an impenetrable mystery.

13. Greene and Hudson, *op. cit.,* p. 189.

Kant's moral pessimism is nevertheless compatible with a certain moral optimism. Kant would perhaps not deny that the sum total of the evil in the world surpasses the amount of pleasure and joy allotted to man, but he would not conclude from this that life is unworthy to be lived. He would insist that we can live a worthy life if we struggle against the moral evil in our breast, and that even misfortune and hardship contribute to the victory which we may win. The moral law is stern and rigorous, but there is victory at the end, even though this end looms only in the infinite distance and entangles the thinking mind in insoluble contradictions. We are never permitted to despair either of ourselves or of the world, neither are we allowed to believe that we can ever reach perfection. Kant depicts man as hovering between the extremes of ignorance and knowledge, of good and evil, of God and Satan (although he does not believe in Satan as a person). But man is not a hybrid in which the opposites disappear by neutralizing each other; rather he participates in their antagonism and is therefore divided against himself. Man experiences to the full the opposition which is the mark of himself as well as it is characteristic of the world in which he lives; in the face of this opposition he has to develop himself and form his Weltanschauung.

III

Ethical Subjectivism

V<small>OLUNTARISM</small> and dualism determine a third facet of Kant's Weltanschauung: its subjectivism. Like voluntarism and dualism this third trait is basically ethical, and indeed it is because of its thoroughly ethical character that both voluntarism and dualism are bound up with it. If the moral will is the center of the human self—if this self centers in morality—and if morality is the center of Weltanschauung, then this Weltanschauung must be subjective, for the human self is human just to the extent to which it is the self of a willing and thinking subject differing fundamentally from all objects that can be willed or thought. Even the moral faith which ensues from the basic moral aspect of life and the world is subjective. Although it is faith not in man but in God, it is nevertheless not a faith in any object or objective entity but in the supreme subject, in the absolute self. This is the reason why God cannot be known in a theoretical and objective way, but only in an ethical, i.e., subjective way.

However, it is not easy to understand how the subject as an ethical self is related to the subject as theoretical intellect or understanding, or how Kant's ethics supplements his theory of knowledge. It is difficult to understand how both ethics and epistemology are integrated with each other and how they constitute one consistent whole. The usual explanation is that the subjectivism of Kant's ethical Weltanschauung is based upon the subjectivism of his epistemological theory which he calls "transcendental idealism." In order to examine this thesis we must turn to the problem of the inner relation between the two types of subjectivism—the ethical and the transcendental one. We must ask which of the two is more characteristic of Kant's Weltanschauung, and which of the two is dominant in the fabric of his feeling and thought. All I have said so far leads one to suspect that the ethical subjectivism is more significant and decisive than the epistemological or transcendental. We shall see that this is indeed so.

If morality is possible at all, the duality of nature and freedom must exist, and its existence must be a limitation of knowledge. Freedom cannot be a quality or property of the subject in the sense in which colors, powers, or potentialities are the qualities or properties of objects. Man is not "free" as the possessor of a "natural" property; he is not free as a result of some natural endowment, but he ought to will and to act as a free subject. He ought to will and to act as a subject in the proper sense, since freedom belongs to the subject (person) and never to an object which is impersonal. This contrast is a precondition of morality. The contrast between theoretical (scientific) knowledge and practical (moral) volition, or between theoretical and practical reason, is likewise such a precondition. Practical reason does not know objects, it does not know nature; it knows rather the purposes of the will, its norms, its goal. The kind of knowledge which is appropriate in the field of the sciences—objective, theoretical, impersonal knowledge—cannot be applied in the fields of willing and acting. The two fields limit each other. This essay therefore set out with the thesis that Kant acknowledges the validity of both science and morality in principle and that this dual acknowledgment is the root of his entire philosophy. We can now see that this same acknowledgment requires the basic subjectivism found in his philosophy.

The theoretical knowability of nature is correlative with the objectivity of the natural phenomena, whereas the subjectivity of the moral will is correlative with the practical character of aims and ends, purposes and norms, imperatives and ideals. This contrast is not resolvable as long as morality exists. Nature has to be restricted so that the moral will has a field of its own; theoretical knowability itself has to be restricted so that freedom can grow. The concept of a limited realm called nature springs therefore from the ethical spirit of Kant's Weltanschauung; it springs from its voluntaristic, dualistic, and subjectivistic features. If practical, i.e., moral reason did not differ from theoretical, i.e., scientific reason in that the former directs the will while the latter conditions the sensible world, the whole opposition between freedom and nature (i.e., the realm of necessity in the sense of causal order) or between the moral and the physical law would never arise. This opposition follows from Kant's ethical subjectivism. It is this subjectivism which restricts the sphere of both objectivity and of natural objects and at the same time refuses to allow nature to exhaust the whole of existence.

It is true that the whole of existence does include both nature and freedom, objects and subjects, the theoretical and the practical. If this whole realm could be known theoretically—if science could be extended to include the moral life—if, in other words, we as subjects were only another kind of object (as psychology, especially in its behavioristic form, makes us believe), then ethical subjectivism would not be an ultimate truth. But in this case ethical voluntarism and ethical dualism would also have to be excluded from metaphysics, and instead there would ensue a speculative intellectualism and monism, a metaphysical naturalism and objectivism. We have seen that Kant denies this possibility most emphatically. Nature has to be restricted for the sake of freedom. The "whole realm of existence" cannot be theoretically known (in the way proposed by a speculative and metaphysical monism). The moral will and moral action are independent of natural causality; they do not belong to the phenomena subject to physical necessity. If either one of the two opposites, nature and freedom, has a legitimate claim to be regarded as a key to the comprehension of the whole realm of existence, it is not nature—the sphere of the objects—that is to be so regarded, but freedom—the sphere of the subjects. Not a scientific objectivism but only an ethical subjectivism would be adequate for comprehending the whole. Such a comprehension, however, is altogether impossible, precisely because moral reason is not theoretical or speculative, not metaphysical, that is, not objective but subjective. Moral reason regulates the life of persons, it does not conceive or contemplate all things as a whole.

From the point of view of ethical subjectivism we can now understand the doctrine of epistemological subjectivism. If it is true that practical reason regulates the life of the will and the realm of moral existence, is it not possible that theoretical reason (or intellect) regulates the realm of natural existence, in so far as this realm is regular at all? This indeed is the core of Kant's famous thesis that the intellect prescribes its laws to nature, and this in turn is the gist of his transcendental idealism or phenomenalism. This phenomenalism is the outcome of his ethical subjectivism. Nature depends in the last analysis, not on the theoretical subject by virtue of its subjective forms or categories of the understanding, but primarily on the moral subject as being in the center of Kant's Weltanschauung. Epistemological subjectivism is a consequence of the ethical and not the reverse.

The limitation of nature as the realm of causal necessity and mathematical order is thus a consequence of moral freedom and a postulate of moral reason. Fichte has emphasized (and even overemphasized) this point by transforming Kant's ethical Weltanschauung into an ethical metaphysics; nature is, as he says, nothing but the "material of duty." Kant is more critical and cautious here as elsewhere; he does not base nature on the moral imperative by deriving the logical forms of the natural order from the idea of freedom and selfhood. If that were possible ethical subjectivism would turn into a speculative theory, a possibility which Kant expressly denies. The "primacy of practical reason" must not be extended (and thereby falsified) by making it the principle of a theoretical (metaphysical) knowledge of the Absolute Ego. Kant rejects this Fichtean presumption. The duality of nature and freedom cannot be theoretically understood or derived from a supreme principle, even if this principle were freedom itself, which indeed does limit nature. This limitation is expressed in the doctrine of transcendental idealism. This doctrine answers the question of how the human intellect is able to discover laws of nature or how nature (the realm of objects) can be known objectively by the thinking subject.

The answer rests upon the sovereignty of reason over nature, and this sovereignty is the result of ethical subjectivism. Even the expression "the intellect prescribes to nature its laws" has a "practical" connotation, for prescribing is a kind of practical action. Kant interprets the relation between theoretical reason (or understanding) and nature by analogy to the relation between practical reason and will. The logical forms, i.e., the highest principles of the natural order, are conceived as norms, rules, regulative concepts—all these terms play a decisive role in the *Critique of Pure Reason*. And all these terms indicate that Kant interprets the operation and function of reason, even in the theoretical field, along the lines of ethical legislation; he alludes directly in one passage to the idea that the root of reason as such is practical. In that passage Fichte may have found the courage of his ethical speculation. Nature indeed depends upon reason, for it is rational and scientifically knowable only on this account. Reason, be it practical or theoretical, is legislator in both fields, but the idea of legislation itself is a practical one. In this way the ethical subjectivism is also victorious in epistemology, although Kant avoids Fichte's exaggerations.

The subjectivism of reason leads to the thesis that the objects, inasmuch as they are scientifically comprehensible, are conditioned by the subject, i.e., by reason. Without this theoretical subjectivism objective truth cannot be discovered: objectivity depends on subjectivity, for without a subject that knows there are no objects to be known. Subjective knowledge is not the opposite of objective knowledge, rather knowledge as knowledge is always an operation or an activity of the thinking subject, and the subjectivity of knowledge does not preclude it from being objective, but, on the contrary, it makes its objectivity possible and meaningful. Objectivity means rationality and thus subjectivity. This subjectivity should not be confused with the so-called "subjectivity" of the human senses or indeed with any psychological or physiological theory whatsoever. In Kant's epistemology the term "subjectivism" always points exclusively to the thinking subject, to the "transcendental," i.e., the "ruling" or "commanding" understanding, to sovereign reason. Kant's subjectivism therefore should not be interpreted by any comparison with Locke, Berkeley, or Hume; it is totally different from the doctrine that knowledge consists of "subjective" impressions and ideas. Just as Kant's concept of the subject is inseparably connected with the concept of reason, likewise his subjectivism is by no means psychological but logical and ethical. Kant's ethical subjectivism is predominant throughout his philosophy.

In the *Critique of Pure Reason* Kant calls space and time "forms of pure intuition." None of his theses is more open to misinterpretation and none was more widely attacked or defended than this famous doctrine. Kant conceives of space and time primarily as principles of mathematical knowledge both pure and applied. Nature can be known mathematically because space and time are both forms of human intuition and therefore forms of nature herself. Space and time are subjective and therefore objective too, for it is the knowing subject which is the legislator here. Space and time are the forms that order the sphere of objects which can be known mathematically. The doctrine of space and time is invoked for the purpose of explaining the possibility of mathematical physics, but it has an ethical background and an ethical implication. The knowing subject is able to encompass the sphere of objects because it is on the same level as the moral subject. Man as a subject is not a mere product of nature because, and to the extent that, he is a moral agent: free and autonomous, the author and initiator of his own actions. He is what he is in both fields, the theoretical and the practical, because he is the representative of pure reason or because pure reason is embodied in him as a subject. Thus the subjectivism of the epistemological interpretation of nature has its roots in the subjectivism of the ethical interpretation of man.

Man as a moral will and moral person does not belong to the objective world, he does not belong to the world of objects—he is superior to the whole spatial-temporal order. This is the meaning of his being a subject. As such, he is superspatial as well as supertemporal. He belongs to a purely intelligible or (to employ the Greek term) *noumenal* sphere. In this fact lies the foundation of his moral dignity. The subjectivism of nature therefore does not mean that man's psychological or physiological constitution transforms nature by the process of knowledge or that man adapts the external world to his internal conditions, thus, in a sense, anthropomorphizing it. On the contrary, nature is rationalized by the knowing subject and thus elevated to its true essence or to its essential truth. Nature has no truth outside, or apart from, its rationality. Science comprehends the objects as they really and truly are. It is the intellectual dignity of man corresponding to his moral dignity which enables the scientist to purify the sensible world so that it can be interpreted in mathematical symbols. In this respect Kant's doctrine is not a subjectivism at all.

The subjectivism of Kant's epistemology as well as that of his ethics heightens and exalts the significance of man. As the ethical realm is not degraded or debased by the subjectivity of the moral will, the realm of scientific knowledge is likewise not impaired by the subjectivity of nature. Instead, it is rational sovereignty and power which is manifest in both fields and which corresponds to the majesty of truth and morality. Nature is essentially subjective; a non-subjective nature would be a non-rational nature—it would not be nature at all. For what we call nature is determined by the rational character which makes scientific investigation and the foundation of scientific explanation possible. A non-subjective knowledge of nature is absurd. If our knowledge in so far as it is rational is subjective, then nature too is necessarily subjective; but whether there is anything that exists beyond the horizon of the subject and of subjective knowledge at all (as Kant's expression "thing-in-itself" seems to suggest) is another question. By no means can this transcendent thing be an "object" in the sense of scientific objects and in the sense required by scientific objective knowledge.

The conclusion, therefore, that the epistemological subjectivism does not restrict the possibility of knowing objects is justified. If this possibility were restricted, such restriction would concern not the knowledge of the objects *qua* objects of knowledge but rather the knowledge of the objects in so far as they are more than objects of knowledge. But what else can objects be except objects? In what sense can they surpass objectivity and be something more than objects of knowledge? The theory of scientific knowledge as Kant develops it in the *Critique of Pure Reason* cannot satisfactorily answer these questions; they transcend the concept of the object as much as they transcend the entire horizon of epistemology. They point to those problems which Kant regards as insoluble precisely because they cannot be solved by means of epistemological thought. If the sphere of objects is subjective in the sense of being a restricted sphere, this must mean that objects (nature as such) belong to a wider realm, that they are a fragment or segment of a larger whole.

It is not then the subjectivity of knowledge which is

the restricting factor, but rather that the objective sphere itself is restricted precisely because it is objective. Nature as such is not the whole; it is not fully known or knowable by scientific methods because by such methods it is not known in the perspective of the whole. Science is restricted because it investigates and explains the objects in a merely objective way, i.e., one which is not meta-objective: science investigates and explains in a merely physical and empirical, not in a meta-physical and speculative way. Nature as a restricted realm is truly known by science as it really (objectively) is, but this type of knowledge is restricted. In so far as nature is envisaged from the perspective of the whole of reality, the natural sciences cannot know it, and the theory of scientific knowledge (i.e., epistemology) cannot even define what is meant by nature in this sense. Scientific knowledge is subjective just because it is scientific and not speculative.

Subjectivism thus conceived implies the method of scientific rationality, and, since this method restricts the mode of knowledge, subjectivism also implies that in such knowledge we do not have absolute knowledge. We would know nature absolutely if we could know it, not merely by scientific means, but also by knowing either the whole of reality or knowing reality through the concept of this whole. Schelling, later on, constructed such an absolute knowledge of nature in his famous "philosophy of nature." Kant, on the contrary, denied such a philosophy just as he denied Fichte's metaphysics of an Absolute Ego. We do not know, and can never know, what nature ultimately is, how it is ultimately one with freedom or how it looks from the point of view not of man but of God. Subjectivism, like voluntarism and dualism, figures in Kant's Weltanschauung precisely because it imposes a restriction upon our power of comprehension; it is the ethical root of subjectivism which brings about this imposition, since it demands that there be "room for freedom." The contrast between freedom and nature, between subject and object, is essential to the primacy of moral reason and must not be obliterated by any claim to a higher knowledge. Nature can be known only subjectively, for if it could be known absolutely freedom could likewise be known absolutely. But then morality would be destroyed, for morality cannot survive inclusion in an absolute system. Where it is so included (as in the case of Hegel's system) its distinctiveness is lost and man's moral dignity is thereby eclipsed.

The real opposite of subjectivism is therefore not objectivism but absolutism. Kant's epistemological subjectivism does not restrict scientific knowledge because it denies its objectivity, but because it denies its absoluteness. The objects are known by physics and the natural sciences as they objectively are, but they are not known as they are "in God." We do not see things in God, as Berkeley claims that we do. Our sense perception and our intellectual conception, even at best, do not penetrate into the divine mystery of all things; instead, they are human powers, and, being human, they are both subjective and objective but never absolute or divine. The mutual dependence of subjectivity and objectivity rests upon the split of man's consciousness into the consciousness of nature, i.e., the objective world and the consciousness of his own self and the realm of persons. It is because of morality and freedom that this split cannot and must not be overcome. The duality of science and action must be preserved at all costs. Subjectivity and objectivity are bound together just as the knowing subject is bound up with the objects known.

That is the reason why Kant's epistemology culminates in the famous dictum: "The conditions for the possibility of the experience of the objects are at the same time the conditions for the possibility of the objects themselves." In this principle the identity of the objectivity of the objects and of the subjectivity of knowledge with respect to their supreme conditions is directly emphasized. As long as we stay within the confines of Kant's epistemology, we can never transcend the limitation of this mutual relation of objects and subject. Kant refuses to allow any concept of an Absolute which would be both objective and subjective as is the case with the Absolute in the systems of Schelling and Hegel.

Kant's theory of knowledge definitely separates the human and the divine. We are human and, that is to say, finite, because our knowledge of the objects is separated from the knowledge of God and, in this sense, relinquishes any claim to final truth. The truth of science is forever finite and restricted just as man's moral achievements are forever finite and imperfect. The third division of the *Critique of Pure Reason,* the so-called "Transcendental Dialectic," is dedicated to the explicit demonstration of these limits of theoretical knowledge.

The limitation of knowledge is not to be attributed to the inadequacy of the understanding alone; it is rather the consequence of the mutual relation of object and subject. It is the consequence of the primacy of the subject, that is, of ethical subjectivism. The world as a whole, the human soul, and God cannot be known by the human understanding, because they can never be made the objects of sense perception and theoretical conception in the same way as can natural phenomena. They are names for something that transcends the "forms" of sense intuition as well as of rational intellection, and they are not in space and time as the objects of physics are. They are in the proper sense metaphysical and they therefore resist the methods of physics and of the finite intellect as such. They are not conditioned by the same categories that condition everything natural, and they are in that sense supranatural. They cannot be investigated, analyzed, and subjected to experiment as can the objects of science. They transcend the scientific horizon and are, in this sense, "transcendent." The relation between object and subject which enables man to know objects is no longer valid here.

The subjective conditions which give the understanding its strength and power in the field of the natural sciences are the duality of object and subject, the dependence of the objects upon the subject, the spatiality and temporality of the natural phenomena. These are no longer conditions of those transcendent "objects" which Kant calls "Ideas" in order to distinguish them from the phenomena of nature. The world as a whole is not a phenomenon in the same sense as all events and substances within the world are phenomena. The soul is not an entity capable of being experienced in the same way as are psychological data and processes. And God—the Idea of an entity which comprises all entities and is more real than any simple thing—is beyond all possible experience and beyond the horizon of all possible objective knowledge.

Only a pre-Kantian dogmatism could hold that God, soul, and world are knowable by rational means. In that sense many philosophical systems, even at present, are still pre-Kantian in a systematic, though not in a historical, sense. Indeed, all naturalism of whatever kind is pre-Kantian, the naturalism of Bergson no less than that of Alexander or Driesch, the naturalism of Marx as well as that of Feuerbach or Strauss, although all these thinkers lived after Kant. None of them understood the truth behind Kant's subjectivism, and therefore all of them disregarded his warning and considered themselves justified in setting aside the limits which he had imposed. These limits, rightly considered, are no limits imposed upon human knowledge from outside. It is not correct to say, as has been repeatedly done by critics, that Kant in the "Dialectic" taught agnosticism or rational resignation; at least, it is not correct to say this in the sense in which Kant's critics generally have. In warning us to be wary of any dogmatic metaphysics and in proving that reason is not endowed with the power of knowing the world, the soul, and God, Kant certainly does away with a certain type of knowledge. But the question is, what type?

Clearly, Kant rejects that philosophical knowledge which tends to deal with the transcendent Ideas as if they were concepts of finite things belonging to the spatial-temporal world and subject to the same rational categories which control the substances and processes within that world. But to renounce such knowledge is by no means to espouse what has been called agnosticism. On the contrary, it simply excludes spurious knowledge and dispels the illusion of a knowledge which is really no knowledge at all. Kant's rejection of metaphysical knowledge actually guards against the falsification of the true nature of transcendent Ideas. Only if the world, the soul, and God were finite things would such knowledge as Kant rejects be possible; but then they would not be what they are, they would not represent a sphere which definitely transcends nature. Kant's restriction is therefore in no way a statement of resignation but, on the contrary, a triumph of clarification.

It is the inadequacy of objective knowledge and even the nature of an object itself, rather than the inability of the subject, which entails the limitation of knowledge in relation to the transcendent Ideas. It belongs to the nature of an object to be finite, conditioned, and incomplete just as it belongs to the nature of objective knowledge not to reach the Infinite, the Unconditional, and the Perfect. This is the reason why God and the world cannot be known as nature can. Thus, Kant does away with limits rather than imposing them, because he frees the Ideas from the bondage in which they were placed by metaphysical dogmatism. It is only subsequent to this that Kant reaches intellectual resignation. It is not because the intellect is unable to comprehend the transcendent Ideas as it does scientific objects, but because being human the intellect is finite and therefore unable to understand the reality of the transcendent Ideas. In this sense the Ideas are "mere" Ideas, i.e., subjectively conditioned.

To be sure, science investigates and comprehends the reality of its objects, and, seen from this standpoint, science succeeds in its own field better than metaphysics does in the field of the Ideas. The objects are accessible because they are controlled by the intellect; the Ideas are transcendent because they transcend the intellect. It is for this reason that objective knowledge of the Ideas is not only impossible but not even to be desired. The Ideas transcend the whole sphere of objectivity with regard to both objects and objective knowledge. Still, there is a defect in knowing them merely as Ideas, but it is not the defect of a subjective rather than an objective knowledge, but the defect of a subjective, that is a finite, knowledge. This defect characterizes the limitation of the human intellect and stamps that intellect as human. A divine intellect would be able to understand the Ideas not merely as Ideas but in their reality. But even so, the divine intellect would not know the Ideas as objects in an objective way, as nature is known to us, but it would know them "face to face," i.e., in their fulness and totality.

Kant develops the hypothetical idea of the divine intellect in his third *Critique,* the *Critique of Judgment.* He conceives this intellect as not being discursive like the human intellect which cannot grasp truth without moving around it, taking one step at a time, stopping to analyze and then to reconstruct. The divine intellect, on the contrary, is intuitive and knows the truth in one glance. The Ideas, inasmuch as they are mere Ideas, i.e., Ideas separated from reality, are a product of human understanding. This separation is a result of discursive thinking and, in that sense, it is merely subjective. The divine intellect in its knowing of the truth does not have to proceed one step at a time, it does not need to separate reality and Idea, for it is infinite and unrestricted. God, and God alone, knows the full truth at a glance. He alone knows himself, the world, and the soul. Man knows only the *Idea* of God, the world, and the soul. It is this which constitutes the inevitable and definitive limitation of human knowledge. One can say that the entire separation of object and subject as well as that of theoretical and practical reason is only human; in the comprehension of God it does not exist. How far this comprehension can be fathomed by us is a difficult question which I will discuss later on. Here I only want to emphasize that the subjectivism of Kant's epistemology is in accord with his general view which stresses the limitation of man for the sake of his moral task and life.

In the divine intellect nature and freedom, object and subject, are not separated as they are in the human. Since man is basically a moral being, this separation is necessary. He could not strive and struggle, he could not be a responsible person, if this separation were not characteristic of his human lot. The epistemological subjectivism of the transcendent ideas is based therefore, as is that of objective knowledge and the objects themselves, on the ethical subjectivism of Kant's Weltanschauung. Not the knowing, but the morally willing and acting, subject is subject in that distinctive sense which sets man off as finite in contrast to the infinity of God. Moreover, the epistemological principle of limitation, the so-called "agnosticism" of Kant, is in perfect agreement with the biblical Weltanschauung which also separates God and man in principle and which likewise holds that men cannot fathom the mystery of God just because God can be known only in so far as he reveals himself. Kant is less not more agnostic than the Bible, since he at least admits a certain comprehension by means of reason alone, though not of God himself, but of the Idea of God. In this comprehension practical reason—the reason of the willing and acting subject—has predominance, not the reason of the scientific or speculative intellect.

Man is, in the true sense, a subject only in so far as he wills and acts. This is true even of the subject which seeks scientific knowledge, for we can know nature only through voluntary and active investigation of her phenomena. Science never comes to an end; it is a dynamic activity (not a process) precisely because the scientist himself is, above all, a human subject, finite and imperfect as long as he does not see and grasp the full and total truth. If he could ever reach this goal, he would no longer be a scientist, a human subject, but he would be "like God." The object of theoretical knowledge exists as an object only within the horizon of the human consciousness, whereas the object of the will never exists at all for it is ever fleeting, ever to be realized but never real. Its realization is an eternal task. From the practical perspective theoretical knowledge itself is determined by the will—the will to know the truth. And seen from this perspective, knowing, like all other human activity, is never ending; truth—its supreme and ultimate "object"—is never grasped. This is the deepest insight in Kant's epistemological subjectivism.

On the basis of this insight the transcendent Ideas assume the significance of intellectual tasks never completely fulfilled and forever standing at the horizon of human science, while science itself takes on significance as an approach toward the solution of these tasks. In this way, ethical subjectivism is not only the background but even the very life of science. Science is basically an ethical undertaking; this is its ultimate and most exalted conception. The ethical ideal thus penetrates the theoretical sphere itself and appears within it as its supreme master and interpreter. Kant speaks directly of the Ideal of (theoretical) Reason as the culmination of the entire theory of knowledge. It is only now that the whole depth of Kant's subjectivism opens before our eyes: it is not that we know the objects only subjectively, but that our very knowledge is part and parcel of our moral existence. This is the innermost essence of his subjectivism.

Epistemology, then, finally becomes a province of Kant's ethical Weltanschauung. All interpreters of Kant (and they are in the majority) who believe that the epistemology is the center, the ground, the very essence of Kant's philosophy, and that his ethics represents only a subsidiary venture, an appendix or merely a part besides other parts in his thought, ignore the inner structure of the whole. While Kant did not go as far as Fichte, who constructed his system with ethics as its root and as its goal, Kant did pave the way toward such a system. He avoided the consequence drawn by Fichte because he was not as willing as Fichte to subordinate the theoretical activity of scientific knowledge exclusively to ethical thought. He was aware of a certain self-dependence of nature, and, as we have seen, he never abandoned the indissoluble duality of nature and freedom, and therefore of theory and practice, of intellect and will. Consequently, he maintained the duality of epistemology and ethics and did not proceed to the establishment of an all-embracing system. In his Weltanschauung we can find an unsystematic, even an antisystematic tendency. It is precisely because of this feature that it is more accurate to speak of Kant's Weltanschauung and not of his system.

The antagonism of object and subject is an integral and enduring factor in Kant's Weltanschauung. Neither speculation nor moral faith can do away with this antagonism. Kant's philosophy, revolutionary as it is, preserves a great deal of common sense, of English empiricism. Kant understands even better than the empiricists themselves what the nature of experience is. Science depends upon experience because the subject operative in scientific investigation is human and finite and, for the same reason, the objects are finite, being objects of a finite knowledge or phenomena. The logical impossibility of replacing experience by any rational construction or intuitive insight rests upon the ethical impossibility of replacing action by speculation. The ethical goal can be attained only approximately, and this is true of the cognitive goal as well. Both are goals, because in both cases the willing subject is the subject in the most appropriate sense. Although cognition of the truth is, precisely speaking, at its goal, science is infinitely separated from it. For cognition as well as action is always incomplete and fragmentary. The incomplete character of the objective world and objective knowledge thus depends upon the limitation or imperfection of the ethical subject.

Nature as the totality of objects corresponds to man as the subject of objective knowledge. Nature itself is as finite (i.e., incomplete and imperfect) as man is, for one correlates with the other and cannot be conceived without the other. The finite human understanding of the ethical subject requires, as its counterpart, just such a finite world as the one in which we exist. This world is conditioned and even "created" by the human understanding, i.e., by the intellect of a being that is not creator but creature. Many philosophical systems have conceived of theoretical reason as being infinite, perfect, and divine. Kant, on the other hand, thinks of theoretical reason as being finite, imperfect, and human, because he holds that the intellect and the will are on the same level. If it is true that the forms of nature are rooted in man's intellect, then it follows that they are also indirectly rooted in man's will, although Kant avoids logically deriving any of these forms from the will.

Is such a view not somewhat precarious? Is it not absurd to interpret nature as the creation of the human intellect? Is not man rather a creature of nature herself? And is it not possible to assume that an infinite and unrestricted intellect would know nature as it is "in itself," i.e., free from the imperfections which attach to human knowledge? Is it not much more natural to grant such a possibility and thus to think of nature herself as infinite, perfect, and divine? Is not nature the creator while man is the creature, and does not nature thus ultimately coincide with the infinite, perfect, and divine intellect? Such a view would issue in an absolute subjectivism superior to Kant's ethical subjectivism because the subject would no longer be man but God; it would be a meta-ethical subjectivism.

Only this absolute subjectivism, so it seems, would no longer stand in contrast to any epistemological objectivism but would be identical with it, because only such an intellect would penetrate the objects absolutely, thereby bridging any chasm between cognition and absolute truth.

However, such a view is excluded by the very principles of Kant's Weltanschauung. The idea of nature as no longer restricted leads precisely to that kind of speculation which Kant regards as both fallacious and detrimental to morality. It leads to an uncritical, that is to say, dogmatic, identification of nature and God, of object and subject. It totally abandons the solid ground of human experience and thought. Nature freed from all restrictions is no longer nature as investigated and understood by science; scientific knowledge freed from all restrictions is no longer scientific knowledge such as we alone can acquire. When the restrictions are set aside, striving and error disappear and with their disappearance the phenomenal world itself must go. The total identity of subject and object, of nature and God, implies total destruction of all our concepts; it is the total night in which all differentiation and therefore all comprehension vanishes.

Kant calls the possibility which is an impossibility for us a regulative ideal, i.e., a concept which signifies the limit of all insight. The regulative ideal is peculiar in that its content is no longer commensurate with the content of all concepts within the limit; and yet its content cannot be conceived except as the limiting case of all those concepts. The numbers zero and infinity are thus border cases of the numerical system. They are numbers in so far as we can conceive them, and yet they no longer compare with all other numbers. When we use them in calculus we notice that they do not obey the arithmetical rules; they are abnormal numbers and yet they are nothing but numbers. The epistemological borderline case is akin to the numerical one. It marks the maximum of knowledge which can be conceived in terms of knowledge attainable to us alone, and yet it is unattainable in those terms. Our knowledge is conditioned by only a partial identity of object and subject, namely, a partial identity of the conditions or forms of the objects and of the intellect, and by a partial incongruity of matter and form in the objects and of sense and reason in the subject. When this approaches the vanishing point as is the case in total identity (the borderline case of knowledge) then the concepts of subject and object, of form and matter, are themselves done away with and consequently even the concept of their identity becomes incomprehensible. Since to know means to subjectify what is objective, it follows that we do no longer know anything when subject and object are regarded as identical.

The very concept of knowledge is therefore bound up with Kant's ethical subjectivism; only ethically subjective knowledge can be understood as knowledge. The theory of knowledge ends where ethical subjectivism ends, for they are mutually dependent upon each other. Only a world subjectively restricted can become the object of knowledge, only a subject likewise restricted can be conceived as the knowing subject.

But does this not imply that the only conceivable knowledge is that of the natural sciences and that the only conceivable object of knowledge is nature? In a sense this is really Kant's conviction. Wherever Kant speaks of objective knowledge, of theoretical reason and so on, he always has in mind the natural sciences. But what about the knowledge of his own critical philosophy? How does the theory of knowledge comprehend philosophical cognition itself? Kant does not philosophize about his philosophy. He inquires into the spheres of the natural sciences and of morality, into art and religion, but he hardly ever touches upon the problem of philosophy itself. Kant has no epistemology of philosophical knowledge, and some of his difficulties are connected with this defect. Like most great discoverers he was naive with respect to the nature of the very instrument which helped him to make his discovery. It is not my intention to correct Kant or to fill the gap in his system.[1] I must, however, discuss one important concept which in many ways illuminates this gap without filling it: the concept of the thing-in-itself.

1. A German thinker, Emil Lask, who was killed in World War I, tried to fill this gap in his book, *Die Logik der Philosophie und die Kategorienlehre* (Tübingen: J. C. B. Mohr [Paul Siebeck], 1911).

IV

Ethical Phenomenalism

Is NOT the thing-in-itself precisely that object which is supposed to transcend the limits of knowledge and which, therefore, cannot be grasped in any but a subjective way? Is not the thing-in-itself that transcendent reality from which we are forever cut off by an insurmountable barrier? Is not the pre-Kantian conception of knowledge thus introduced anew into epistemology? Does this not mean that we return to an epistemological conception which insists that the object must be absolutely independent of the subject and that the subject does not condition the object in any respect? All the considerations of the preceding chapter safeguard us from falling victim to such an erroneous interpretation. As long as we stay within the limits of the Kantian epistemology, such a false argument is unlikely. When we leave epistemology behind, the whole contrast between object and subject is no longer valid. The thing-in-itself can therefore even be regarded as an object of divine knowledge.

The real meaning of the concept under consideration

is not epistemological at all. It is founded on the ethical contrast between nature and freedom and derives its power from this moral source. Ethics, as it were, demands the limitation of epistemology, and this means that epistemology is being limited in the interests of morality. The thing-in-itself, seemingly an object transcending knowledge, becomes instead the objective of striving; it corresponds not so much to the knowing as to the willing subject. Kant had to insist upon the limitation of knowledge and thereby upon the unknowable thing-in-itself for the sake of the realm of freedom in which the will unfolds itself. The objectivity of the thing-in-itself thus discloses itself not as the objectivity of a new object of knowledge but as the objectivity of duty—the object of the will. Despite the fact that the will is even more subjective than the intellect, this new objectivity is of a higher grade than the objectivity of nature and of natural knowledge just because it points to the supersensible. To be sure the object of the will restricts the realm of merely theoretical objects, but it also enlarges the human horizon. In this way theoretical knowledge is restricted because it does not exhaust the content of the human consciousness. Without the thing-in-itself we could never understand the practical aspect of science, the emphasis placed upon progress, and the significance of the intellectual conscience of the scientist. This ethical element within epistemology which gives knowledge its peculiar subjectivity also leads man to an objectivity superior to all knowledge. It is a symptom of a narrow mind to insist, as some are inclined to do, that theoretical objectivity eclipses morality. It is true that we as moral beings are most impressed by our imperfection and our subjective finitude as an almost unbearable burden. However, it is the same imperfection and the same finitude which also limit our theoretical understanding.

It is the peculiar glory of the ethical to enlarge the mind's horizon to an ever increasing extent and to open up for it a vista of infinity. By leaving natural knowledge with its desire for truth forever unsatisfied, the thing-in-itself bestows a peculiar nobility upon scientific knowledge. The infinite embodies an object never to be possessed and an objectivity transcending any attainable objectivity. The thing-in-itself symbolizes ultimate truth, forever attracting the searching mind from a distance never to be spanned. Every truth actually reached is really penultimate, finite and therefore not satisfying. This is the ultimate reason why Kant calls the object of natural knowledge, phenomenon or appearance. Everything encompassed by science is finite and therefore can be put down as appearance. Every human intellect is limited because the will also must be provided for; the will demands freedom which in turn necessitates limitation of the objective sphere. Thus the objective sphere must be conceived as a phenomenal one.[1] Nature takes on a phenomenal aspect for the sake of morality, and this means that its limitations are postulated by freedom. Nature must appear in such guise, not because man is unable to discover what might be called its reality or actuality, but because man has the moral capacity and duty to will something that is beyond nature. The thing-in-itself is thus the goal of man's moral quest.

Nature ought to be nothing more than appearance; such a view is demanded by the ethical spirit of Kant's Weltanschauung. Schelling, in a poignant passage of his *Philosophical Letters on Dogmatism and Criticism,* makes this same point:[2] "Have you never guessed, however darkly, that it is not the weakness of your reason but rather the absolute freedom of your will which makes the noumenal world inaccessible to any objective power? Have you never guessed that it is not the limitation of your knowledge but rather your unlimited

1. It is at this point that a great many English-speaking interpreters have misunderstood Kant's language by identifying what is here called his "ethical phenomenalism" with a psychological or physiological phenomenalism.

2. F. W. J. von Schelling, *Philosophische Briefe über Dogmatismus und Kriticismus"* (1795), *Werke,* I, 340.

freedom which keeps the objects of knowledge within the confines of mere appearance?" We can never have any knowledge of nature which would not be fragmentary, which would not raise new questions and which would not be problematic and essentially incomplete. Nature in itself is merely appearance because as such it never exists for itself but only for us. It is, as it were, the counterpart of our finite understanding which is finite just because of our supernatural freedom.[3]

At this point we can no longer avoid the question

3. Sometimes it has been held that our knowledge of nature is more than a knowledge of appearance because science transcends the horizon of sense perception and penetrates into the essence of sensible things. This is a typical misinterpretation and one already rejected by Kant himself. If the term "essence" points to that ultimate truth meant by the term "thing-in-itself," then science does not produce a knowledge of the essence of things. [T. M. Greene and H. H. Hudson (trans.), *Religion within the Limits of Reason Alone* (Chicago: Open Court Publishing Co., 1934), p. 58.] Certainly, Kant sometimes used the expression "in-itself" in a loose sense; thus he would say, for example, that science knows nature in its truth and, he would add, "nature-in-itself." Compare the following from the first *Critique:* "When, therefore, we say that the senses represent objects *as they appear,* and the understanding objects *as they are,* the latter statement is to be taken, not in the transcendental, but in the merely empirical meaning of the terms, namely as meaning that the objects must be represented as objects of experience, that is, as appearances in thoroughgoing interconnection with one another, and not as they may be apart from their relation to possible experience (and consequently to any senses), as objects of the pure understanding" *Critique of Pure Reason,* trans. Norman Kemp Smith, p. 274 (A 258 = B 314).

raised at the end of the last chapter: Does philosophy suffer the same restriction as science? Is philosophical truth also to be distinguished from ultimate truth? Is philosophy as well as science forever engaged in a progress which has no end? Must we therefore conclude that philosophy, like science, apprehends appearance and nothing more? Or, in other words, is Kant's phenomenalism to be extended over the whole of human knowledge? This would seem to be absurd because the whole distinction between science and philosophy would then break down and, even worse, philosophy thus restricted would be in no position to set the limits of science. Consequently, the whole enterprise of epistemology as well as of ethics would ultimately be impossible. Yet we are not allowed simply to conclude that philosophy does succeed in knowing the thing-in-itself, or that the thing-in-itself grasped by the philosopher is that unattainable phantom for which science must forever continue to search. Metaphysics prior to Kant thought of the thing-in-itself as its proper object of knowledge; Kant revolutionized this view. He gave up such dogmatic metaphysics by recognizing that the whole relation between the object known and the knowing subject never includes the thing-in-itself. Nevertheless, the problem involved here is not solved by this negative attitude alone, and it is a genuine problem because the relation between object and subject as it exists in science characterizes a concept of finite knowledge only. What then is the ultimate relation between the pre-Kantian dogmatism and the Kantian criticism of the thing-in-itself?

Whatever conception of knowledge may be implied by a theory of philosophical knowledge, two things are clear: first, such a theory cannot deny the validity of scientific truth and, second, the basic distinction between scientific and philosophical knowledge must not be obliterated. In other words, the relationship between object and subject must be maintained, but it must not be applied to philosophical knowledge. The theory of scientific knowledge is a theory of the relation between subject and object, but the theory itself must not be understood as one more instance of this same relationship but rather as an example of self-knowledge. It is true that the knowing subject makes itself an object of inquiry, but in so doing the very term "object" changes its meaning and takes on the meaning of "subject-become-object" in which both are identical. Thus, the thing-in-itself can no longer be an object in the sense of the old metaphysics.

The object in the epistemological sense is always dependent upon the knowing subject and is thereby phenomenal, whereas the subject, even if it is made to stand in the position of an object, is not phenomenal but noumenal. In a way, the subject is *a* thing in itself; it is, as Fichte calls it, an ego in itself. Is perhaps *the* thing-in-itself nothing else but the subject? Kant recoils from drawing this conclusion but he approaches it, and Fichte was not completely disloyal to Kant when he insisted that the ultimate conception of the thing-in-itself leads to the idea of an absolute ego. Kant did not go so far because he makes ethics not metaphysics the fundamental discipline. The subject in the true sense is the moral person. The theory of scientific knowledge is overarched, not by the theory of philosophical knowledge or by a metaphysics of an absolute ego, but by the ethical insight that the moral subject does not belong to the phenomenal world but to a realm of freedom.

Kant's philosophy is raised above the level of natural science inasmuch as it understands such knowledge to be knowledge of a morally free subject related to a world of phenomena. However, it would be wrong to conclude from this supremacy and from the insight that nature is only appearance that philosophy is able to reach the thing-in-itself. Although the term "appearance" seems to require the term "reality" as its counterpart, and although one might identify the thing-in-itself with reality in its ultimate sense, nevertheless, there is something in between appearance and reality, and this is the subject to which the objects appear. This subject should not simply be interpreted as being true reality and consequently a thing-in-itself, although in a sense, it takes on the function of the thing-in-itself. Certainly the subject to which the objects appear does not itself appear but is a presupposition or an a priori principle of the phenomenal world. Even so, this principle is not what appears and therefore is not ultimate reality.

In his ethics Kant goes a step further; here he would say that the human will inasmuch as it is subject to the moral law is not merely an appearance but appears to itself. Is the will perhaps the thing-in-itself? Schopenhauer proceeded along such a line, thereby yielding to the temptation to produce a new metaphysics of the will. It is Kant's ethical Weltanschauung which forbids him to take such a step. However, it is true that will or self, as conceived by ethics, points in the direction of the thing-in-itself. Just as the knowing subject stands between the extremes of appearance and ultimate reality (certainly nearer to reality than to appearance), so the morally willing and acting self likewise stands between these extremes but even nearer to ultimate reality. Consequently we must acknowledge a truth in between the merely finite and outer truth of scientific knowledge and the absolute and ultimate truth which science can never reach. This truth would not be as empirical as scientific truth nor as metaphysical as speculative truth. It would not be merely pragmatic, but it would also not be dogmatic; it would be critical and ethical. This is the truth of Kant's philosophy.

Philosophy occupies the middle ground between the two opposite extremes of truth and is thus enabled and entitled to mediate between the age-old antagonists, physics and metaphysics, experimental and speculative knowledge. Kant's philosophy fully recognizes the truth of science and acknowledges the function of experience in contrast to the premature claims of metaphysical systems which claim to possess that truth to which science can never attain. Kant thus assures science of the fulfilment of its highest aspirations (even more surely than any philosopher before or after him had done) by dethroning metaphysical systems. On the other hand, Kant's philosophy claims to have transcended the horizon of science and to have become the heir of metaphysics. Kant regards himself as the custodian of that ultimate knowledge which the metaphysician pretends to possess, but which no human being can ever attain. The realm of the things-in-themselves remains uncomprehended and incomprehensible, although ethical philosophy partly comprehends it as the realm of freedom and thereby mediates between the separated domains of appearance and reality, between that truth which is merely for us and the truth in itself. Here we return to the same antinomy which we met previously in the discussion of ethical dualism. Ethical phenomenalism interprets nature as appearance and the moral will or the ethical subject as thing-in-itself. At the same time, the ethical phenomenalism criticizes such an interpretation as constituting metaphysical knowledge of the thing-in-itself. In the last analysis it remains true that the realm of freedom cannot be fully understood or conceived because it is an objective of the moral will and of the moral faith but not an object of the understanding. Some further considerations should be added in order to show that the thing-in-itself presents what is finally an insoluble problem.

First, we must take note of the distinction between the incomprehensibility of the thing-in-itself and the partial comprehensibility of nature. Natural knowledge is always in the making; discoveries and theories progress toward the whole which can never be grasped because the sum total of partial knowledge is no substitute for knowledge of the whole. Nature seen from the standpoint of knowledge is a restricted realm, whereas the thing-in-itself as the ultimate objective of philosophy is beyond all restriction and therefore demands an equally unrestricted knowledge. The ultimate is without boundaries, except for those which are self-imposed. Inasmuch as philosophy is the science of the ultimate and not of the phenomena only, in so far as it concerns the essence and not the appearance of things, and to the extent to which it desires not a fragment of the whole but its totality, it cannot even approach its goal as natural knowledge can. There is an absolute incommensurability between philosophy and the thing-in-itself. Even in speaking of the contrast between the opposites philosophy shows that its goal is not attained, since the very meaning of the thing-in-itself rigorously excludes all opposition. What we mean by thing-in-itself is precisely an absolute unrelatedness; in regarding it as reality in contrast to appearance we are introducing a relation.

The thing-in-itself as contradistinguished from appearance, from the finite, the subjective, or from anything else, is to that degree itself a finite concept conditioned by its opposite. In this way essence is conditioned by contingency or existence, totality by partiality, the ground by its effect or consequence, substance by accident and so forth. All these concepts are finite to the extent to which they do not grasp the unrelated or the unconditioned. But this, according to Kant, is just our logical and ethical situation. We as human beings can only progress by moving from the appearance to the essence, from the part toward the totality. The thing-in-itself in the last analysis is a goal that we can never reach. Indeed our whole being is a moral goal; we never are what we ought to be, we are always in the making both as agents and as knowers. Phenomenalism just because its perspective is ethical leaves the thing-in-itself in that metaphysical twilight which marks the borderline between knowledge and ignorance. Appearance and reality, essence and existence and similar correlates have an ethical connotation in Kant's Weltanschauung and lose their meaning if deprived of such connotation.

When Kant refuses to give a definition of freedom (he calls freedom an inscrutable power and he speaks of our inability to explain how freedom is possible; see *Fundamental Principles of the Metaphysics of Morals,* and *Religion within the Limits of Reason Alone*)[4] the idea that freedom cannot be known in the same way as the natural phenomena can is uppermost in his mind. Thus he measures philosophical compre-

4. Greene and Hudson, *op. cit.,* p. 158 n.; L. W. Beck (trans.), *Foundations of the Metaphysics of Morals,* in *Critique of Practical Reason and Other Writings in Moral Philosophy* (Chicago: University of Chicago Press, 1949), p. 113.

hension by naturalistic standards, standards not to be applied when knowledge of freedom is at stake. Nevertheless, the main drift of his argument can be justified, for if we could fully understand the realm of moral will and action, we would also be able to grasp the relation between freedom and nature so that our natural knowledge would then cease to be merely natural.

However, the philosophical incomprehensibility of the ultimate truth implies that the ultimate relationship between nature and freedom cannot be known. In both cases the restriction of knowledge does not rest upon the theoretical impossibility of combining free will and natural causality but upon the ethical necessity of opposing freedom to nature. It is just because philosophy culminates in ethics that the opposition between nature and freedom ought not to be transcended, and consequently that the domain of things-in-themselves is to be conceived as the realm of the moral will or of pure practical reason. Inasmuch as Kant tries to give an ethical definition of the essence, in contrast to the appearance, of things, he feels logically compelled to conclude that the realm of freedom itself is as inscrutable as is the ultimate essence of things.

Should we not, by the same token, conclude that nature no less than freedom is incomprehensible in so

far as it is related to the unknown and unknowable?
Is it not arbitrary on the part of Kant to call the objects
of nature phenomena, while he speaks of the free will
as a *causa noumenon,* thus designating appearance as
natural and essence as moral? If the things-in-themselves surpass all cognition, as Kant asserts, would it
not be consistent to include freedom as well as nature
under the title of appearance? Such a line of argument
rests on a merely formalistic basis. Such a point of view
is logical only in a superficial sense; in a deep sense it
is illogical because it neglects the centrality of ethics
and assumes a perspective neutral to the ethical cause.
It is precisely the greatness of Kant that he does not fall
victim to such a speculative formalism, for he flatly
denies the possibility of any trans-ethical philosophy. It
is his studied conviction that the contrast of appearance
and essence, the contrast of phenomenon and noumenon, should be taken as an ethical contrast and nothing else.

His philosophy thus gets beyond a knowledge of appearance just because it is philosophy and not science,
but it falls short of a knowledge of essence just because
it is an ethical philosophy and not a dogmatic metaphysics. When Kant conceives of nature as a phenomenal realm, his intention is not so much psychological
(and not even epistemological), as ethical; nature is

phenomenal because it is nothing but the material of the moral will. Nature is phenomenal not because man looks at it only through his own eyes or through spectacles; such an epistemological phenomenalism would evidently lead to a metaphysical, and this means meta-ethical, phenomenalism. Instead, nature is phenomenal because man as a moral person is never permitted to derive his ultimate ends from nature; on the contrary, he is required to subject nature to his own ultimate ends. Nature is merely phenomenal because it is destitute of ultimate ends and of an absolute meaning; both end and meaning are finally connected with the moral will which uses nature as a means and thereby superimposes the realm of freedom upon nature. The term "appearance" thus gains its full significance only in ethics.

V

Primacy of the Practical

In previous chapters the knowledge of nature was distinguished from the moral will on the basis of their relation to their objects. The knowledge of nature, as we have seen, attains its object, while the will remains forever separated from its goal. Later, however, we observed that this distinction could not be fully maintained, since in the pursuit of scientific knowledge the knowing subject is always at the same time a willing and acting subject. Science is not a timeless possessor of the truth but rather a temporal undertaking proceeding toward truth, although it never reaches truth in an absolutely satisfactory way. This fusion within the scientist of knowledge and will is not merely of a psychological and therefore external character but also of an epistemological importance. It is grounded in the subjectivism of Kant's Weltanschauung; but this subjectivism in turn is of ethical origin and is part of the ethical phenomenalism with which we have been dealing.

Thus we must understand that it is the ethical

Weltanschauung which prompted Kant to discover the peculiar method of his philosophy, a method best called "analytical," because Kant analyzes the several functions of the subject and separates them from each other. Even the separation of subject and object is an outcome of this analytical method, a method dictated by an ethical consciousness which finds it necessary to distinguish ideality and reality, end and means, purpose and action, essence and appearance. The same method prevents Kant from ever reaching or re-establishing the "whole" of these contrasting concepts. Philosophical speculation would be wholly satisfied only if this restitution were possible, if it succeeded in finding the ultimate ground from which these contrasts arise. Only then could philosophy succeed in deriving the opposites from a primordial One and in reuniting them by means of it. But the ethical consciousness and the analytical method (which are mutually interdependent) preclude this ultimate solution. Human reason can understand the world and man only by separating them; this restriction characterizes Kant's entire Weltanschauung.

Earlier we had to acknowledge the fact that the ethical dualism cannot be transcended, now we have to acknowledge the fact that the ethical phenomenalism cannot be transcended either. Were it possible to comprehend or to intuit the appearance as the appearance of an underlying essence, and were it possible, moreover, to express this comprehension or intuition in a discursive, dialectical fashion (as Hegel claims to do), ethical phenomenalism would no longer be ethical, and it would no longer serve the innermost motif of Kant's Weltanschauung. In the speculative system of Hegel the ultimate duality is allowed to be absorbed by an ultimate One, because the contrast of appearance and essence, of phenomenon and noumenon, of things-for-us and things-in-themselves is no longer ethically determined and interpreted, but instead it is understood logically, ontologically, cosmologically, and theologically. Consequently in Hegel's system the essence is no longer opposed to the appearance as the ideal to the real or as the goal to the process or as the "ought" to the "is," but both are inwardly and absolutely united in the ultimate One, whether it is called Idea (as in Hegel's *Logic*) or Mind (as in the *Phenomenology* and the *Encyclopedia*). This One by itself and with itself finally unites all the opposites and all distinctions; it is the unity of Concept and Being, of Idea and Reality, of Knowledge and Will. Such a solution would be anathema to Kant.

Ethical phenomenalism denies the possibility of such an absolute system, since the moral will denies its truth.

There is no ultimate reconciliation in Kant's Weltanschauung because there is an everlasting striving and acting. There is no intellectual intuition that could possibly be at man's disposal; in Kant only the idea of God's incomprehensible way of knowing is characterized in this way. Since no one of the basic metaphysical oppositions can be overcome by thought, the opposition between natural science and critical philosophy can never disappear; there is no place for a "philosophy of nature" in Kant's Weltanschauung.[1]

1. It is true that the *Critique of Judgment* by uniting the opposites of nature and mind, of necessity and freedom, provides at least a measure of such a philosophy. In this last of the great *Critiques* Kant, to a certain extent, accomplishes what appears to be a metaphysical synthesis embracing the products of analytical thinking. The beautiful and the organic represent this synthesis. Kant deals with both in the *Critique of Judgment* from one and the same point of view. It was this work which inspired first Schelling and later Hegel and encouraged them to create their synthetic systems. Within the frame of Kant's Weltanschauung, however, even the *Critique of Judgment* does not alter the primacy of ethical thought and the triumph of the analytical method. It was Schelling who abandoned the ethical phenomenalism and tried to replace it with his naturalistic aestheticism. The idea suggested by Kant that works of art as well as the creatures of organic nature represent the unity underlying the contrast between appearance and essence, or between object and subject, found in Schelling an enthusiastic and original defender. He was fascinated by the possibility of unifying the two spheres of Kant's Weltanschauung by means of a speculative philosophy of art, and he dared to articulate this bold metaphysical vision.

Kant, on the contrary, never yielded to any such temptation. Although he agrees that the masterpiece and the organism provide a bridge between the separated realms of nature and mind, he insists,

The final truth would include both the truth of science and the truth of philosophy, but no human knowledge can ever obtain that truth. In so far as it is conceived as the ultimate truth, it is opposed to the proximate truth which we can know, i.e., it is conceived only from the standpoint of a separation which conforms to the facts of moral life and to the horizon of the moral consciousness.

Philosophy would accomplish its own ultimate task only if it could get beyond all the analytical separations; but in that case it would go beyond ethics itself, something which is both ethically and logically prohibited. An Idea that passes beyond the opposition of the phenomenal and the noumenal sphere may be conceivable

---

nevertheless, that this bridge does not really unify them. Instead, art and the organic are themselves separated from nature and mind in that they form a third realm distinct from the other two. Although the aesthetics of the beautiful and the teleology of the organic do offer a synthesis of what is separated in science and morality, this synthesis has neither the power nor the right to claim metaphysical truth. Ethical dualism and phenomenalism still stand as the final word. Neither art nor life enables us to know the hidden ground of nature and mind—that ultimate essence which would explain and produce its own appearance. On the contrary, both the artistic work and the organic being belong to the world of phenomena.

The *Critique of Judgment,* therefore, in spite of the new vistas it opens and the number of suggestions it offers, limits the horizon just where it was limited before. The final result is the primacy of ethical thought and moral action; ethical phenomenalism proves permanently victorious. It is not the organism but the moral will and moral freedom which must be regarded as the absolute purpose.

as an Idea but its object, its real counterpart, would be beyond human reason. It would be neither phenomenal nor noumenal, and there is no third possibility which we can either experience or understand. Natural science would be perfect only if the appearances could be known as the effects or manifestations of an unconditional ground, but this ground can never be known and its very concept is opposed to the concept of its consequent. When the duality of object and subject is given up, the thinking mind ceases to operate in the manner of the sciences. We cannot even imagine what an object would be that is also subject or what a subject would be that is also object. Here we reach the absolute limit of human knowledge.

We are now fully able to understand what we mean when we think of the concept of the absolute essence and of the thing-in-itself: we mean something ambiguous, something that we cannot comprehend either from the ethical perspective or from a meta-ethical absolute, and therefore from an altogether problematic, point of view. This ambiguity generates the apparent contradiction according to which the sphere of the things-in-themselves is impenetrable by human thought and yet is conceived by Kant as the realm of the ideal and the goal of freedom and of the moral person. If we yield to the temptation of an absolute solution, we endanger ethical comprehension; if we stick to this comprehension we thwart perfect and absolute knowledge. It is Kant's conviction that philosophy can grasp the thing-in-itself only within the limits of ethics, and that it therefore can never grasp absolute, i.e., meta-ethical truth. Kant does not deny that the ethical truth transcends itself, that it points to something beyond itself, and that this truth is not ultimate but only proximate. But the ultimate demand of the thinking mind involves us in unavoidable contradictions. The demand, even as a demand, is conceivable only if we adhere to the separation of an ultimate and a proximate truth, and if we maintain in addition that we are moving from one to the other.

If, however, we conceive the demand in this way, we destroy its meaning since it is just the negation of such a separation which is actually demanded. Within the absolute truth no movement from a proximate to an ultimate knowledge is meaningful. Consequently, the very demand itself involves the mind in an insoluble problem, which we cannot fully grasp even as a problem, although we cannot cease trying to do so. The Idea of an absolute unity of all oppositions, necessary and unavoidable though it is, nevertheless contradicts itself and, what is worse, obliterates the ethical meaning of the oppositions. Thus it destroys the very meaning of philosophical truth and of scientific truth as well. Here the antinomy between the ethical and the religious elements of Kant's Weltanschauung once again comes to the fore, this time in the guise of the antinomy between the proximate and the ultimate truth.

This antinomy is not soluble within Kant's philosophy; it is its necessary limit. Earlier I said that, for Kant, the ultimate in itself must always remain an ultimate for us, and yet this should not really be the case inasmuch as it is an ultimate "in-itself." Now we can grasp more clearly the logical structure of Kant's thesis. Since his phenomenalism is of ethical origin and import, the contrast between the "in-itself" and the "for us" is itself to be ethically interpreted: it is a contrast for us only. The phenomenalism is ethical, that is, subjectivistic. A meta-ethical phenomenalism is not possible because the duality of essence and appearance, of the noumenon and the phenomenon, would then no longer be tenable. The meta-ethical is in no sense objectively in-itself any more than it is subjectively in-itself; it is beyond the alternative of "in-itself" and "for us," beyond the opposition of object and subject, as it is also beyond the opposition of nature and self-hood, of necessity and freedom. It is beyond all possible distinctions and therefore beyond all thought and knowledge. It is not an absolute Object, an absolute Being or an absolute Substance, because these categories of objective thinking are not allowed to enter into the ultimate problem since they cannot solve the final antinomy.

Moreover, the meta-ethical must not be comprehended as an absolute Subject that would objectify itself in nature (as Schopenhauer asserts), nor is it to be regarded as an absolute Mind or Spirit that conceives itself and thereby creates the material world (as Hegel asserts). Instead it represents a definitive barrier even to any attempt at solution; it represents, in the language of religion, the mystery of God. Neither our own nor any kind of knowledge we may imagine can grasp this mystery; the very concept of possible knowledge breaks down when thought tries to penetrate this Unknowable. The ultimate truth is no longer of cognitive value, it is not a truth which any understanding can comprehend because even the distinction between understanding and truth is no longer valid when we reach the "in-itself." The ultimate truth is no longer truth in the sense of science and philosophy; it is in no way a logical truth. It is at this point that theory, be it physical, metaphysical, ontological, or epistemological comes to an end. Only the moral faith of the ever striving and seeking man can embrace it.

The final truth is meta-philosophical, meta-theoretical, meta-theological. By no conceivable method can such truth be apprehended or comprehended. The concept of the Absolute is self-contradictory and no dialectical device can solve this final contradiction. Kant paradoxically agrees with the mystic in this respect, despite the fact that he is otherwise opposed to mysticism. This final contradiction once more characterizes the ethical and critical line of Kant's Weltanschauung in a definitive way. As Plato ends in myth, Kant ends in moral faith. It is the glory of these two thinkers who try to comprehend the totality of experience by their thought that they do not violate what is beyond the power of thought. Thus Kant is able to assert and to maintain that not the intellect but the moral will (and faith based upon the moral consciousness) reaches to the very limit of human existence. He holds that ethics is related to ultimate truth neither through the medium of metaphysics nor through that of religion, but by virtue of its own ultimate validity (just as the natural sciences are related to their relative truth by virtue of an immanent rationality which is the rationality of the empirical objects themselves).

Even the dignity and autonomy of moral reason, however, do not entitle the thinking mind to assume that this reason actually performs what cannot be performed at all by human reason. Instead, moral reason is just as limited as scientific understanding. In spite of the sovereignty and self-dependence of the moral sphere it points to a reality that begins exactly where human reason ends: the reality of God. If we could will as God wills, we could also know as God knows. But not only do our will and our knowledge dwindle in the face of God, but we are not even in the position to truly understand God's knowledge as knowledge or to understand God's will as a will.

A creative and productive intellect and an omniscient intuitive will are self-contradictory concepts. An intellect which creates its contents is no longer an intellect as we experience it, and a will which contemplates is no longer what we know as will; in neither case do we conceive what is meant by an intellect and a will in God. These terms when we use them as means for understanding God transcend the capacity of our thought.

Index of Names

Alexander, Samuel, 78
Aristotle, 27
Augustine, St., 52

Baillie, J. B., 47 n.
Beck, L. W., 21 n., 35 n., 45 n., 54 n.,
    104 n.
Bergson, Henri, 78
Berkeley, George, 69, 75
Bowring, E. A., 36 n.

Cassirer, Ernst, vii
Cohen, Hermann, vii

Descartes, René, 2
Driesch, Hans, 78

Erdmann, J. E., 38 n.

Feuerbach, Ludwig, 78
Fichte, J. G., 37 n., 58, 66, 68, 74,
    85, 99

Galileo, 2
Goethe, J. W. von, 25, 36
Greene, T. M., 23 n., 41 n., 57 n.,
    59 n., 96 n., 104 n.

Haldane, R. B., 15 n.
Haller, A. von, 57 n.
Hegel, G. W. F. von, 47 n., 74, 110,
    111 n., 116
Hudson, H. H., 23 n., 41 n., 57 n.,
    59 n., 96 n., 104 n.
Hume, David, 69

Kemp, J., 15 n.
Kemp Smith, Norman, 96 n.
Kroner, Richard, vi, ix

Lask, Emil, 91 n.
Laotse, 16
Leibniz, G. W., 26
Lessing, G. E., 22
Locke, John, 69

Marx, Karl, 78

Natorp, Paul, vii
Nietzsche, F. W., 12, 16 ff.

Plato, 117

Rickert, Heinrich, vii, 38 n.

Schelling, F. W. J. von, 73, 95, 111 n.
Schiller, J. C. F. von, 20
Schopenhauer, Arthur, 7, 9, 12 ff., 19,
    25, 27, 100, 116
Simmel, Georg, 6, 19 n.
Spinoza, B. de, 26, 27
Strauss, D. F., 78

Tertullian, 52

Vaihinger, Hans, 37 n.

Windelband, Wilhelm, vii, 6